"*Overcoming Compulsive Hoarding* is an excellent resource for those who suffer from compulsive hoarding behavior. I am most grateful to the authors who have undertaken a most challenging task. This sorely needed book is clearly and compassionately written. The authors demonstrate a firm grasp of the subject matter while providing a wealth of practical information. It is a remarkable achievement."

> —Janet Lessem, CSW, MSW, associate clinical professor at Benjamin N. Cardozo School of Law of Yeshiva University

D1040456

Overcoming Compulsive Hoarding

WHY YOU
SAVE & HOW
YOU CAN
STOP

Fugen Neziroglu, Ph.D., ABBP
Jerome Bubrick, Ph.D.
Jose A. Yaryura-Tobias, MD

New Harbinger Publications, Inc.

Distributed in Canada by Raincoast Books

Copyright © 2004 by Fugen Neziroglu, Jerome Bubrick, and Jose A. Yaryura-Tobias
New Harbinger Publications
5674 Shattuck Avenue
Oakland, CA 94609

Cover design by Amy Shoup
Edited by Jessica Beebe
Text design by Tracy Marie Carlson

ISBN-10 1-57224-349-X
ISBN-13 978-1-57224-349-1

New Harbinger Publications' Web site address: www.newharbinger.com

09   08   07

15   14   13   12   11   10   9   8   7

Contents

Foreword

One of comedian George Carlin's most famous monologues is "A Place for My Stuff." In it, he describes hilariously how we use material possessions to define who we are, and how our self-worth is directly connected to either the quantity or the quality of our "stuff." He also raises the possibility that this concern about "stuff" can eventually lead to a situation in which acquiring, housing, and preserving one's stuff can become the only point of one's life.

Compulsive hoarding is all about "stuff" too. But compulsive hoarding is not a quest for status, power, and respect. It is a very serious disorder. Clinical psychologists Fugen Neziroglu and Jerome Bubrick and psychiatrist Jose Yaryura-Tobias do not linger unduly over the as-yet-to-be-resolved question of whether compulsive hoarding is a symptom of obsessive-compulsive disorder or a separate disorder. They raise the question, offer evidence, discuss research-based theories, and then get on to the important work: guiding the reader through treatment.

The authors are recognized experts in the field of obsessive-compulsive spectrum disorders, and their knowledge comes through every bit of the way. Drs. Neziroglu and Yaryura-Tobias are the authors of several books and hundreds of papers on obsessive-compulsive disorders. They have treated thousands of patients. All three authors know what works, and they use their vast knowledge and experience to guide the reader successfully through the treatment process.

Overcoming Compulsive Hoarding is unique in its approach. It is engaging and interactive as well as informative. It's like a seminar with a professor who brings her students to understanding by asking all the right questions rather than lecturing. The authors know exactly what questions to pose. They make a difficult problem surmountable.

The first big question is, are you a hoarder? The authors do not ask this question rhetorically. They expect the reader to answer it by completing a self-assessment and an exercise that distinguishes hoarding from collecting. The follow-up text contains all the information the reader will need to understand the different types of hoarding behaviors. The authors provide questionnaires and exercises designed to pinpoint specific hoarding symptoms.

These exercises, interspersed strategically throughout the book, make the reader a participant, not an observer. You cannot get through chapter 1 without learning whether you are a hoarder or a collector. This engagement and interaction continues in each chapter, so that when you've finished the book, you have already started on your way to recovery.

Drs. Neziroglu, Bubrick, and Yaryura-Tobias discuss treatment options and guide the reader through a step-by-step program that teaches how to attack the clutter itself, how to stop acquiring possessions, how to organize and prioritize so that clutter can't build up again, and, finally, how to prevent a relapse.

This book is much more than a text about hoarding. It is an actual therapy program. If you work along with the authors, you will be well on your way to getting your hoarding problems under control.

> —Patricia B. Perkins, JD
> Executive Director, Obsessive Compulsive Foundation

Introduction

Our knowledge of obsessive-compulsive disorder (OCD) has grown over the past fifteen to twenty years; however, there is still one element of OCD that remains largely unknown. Compulsive hoarding is a fascinating and often misunderstood phenomenon. In a nutshell, *compulsive hoarding* is the acquisition and saving of possessions that have little or no value, or have some perceived value, and that the person has great difficulty discarding.

Hoarders and Their Behaviors

Even though our knowledge of hoarding accumulates every day (no pun intended), we are continually attempting to understand the damaging effects it has on its victims and their families. Within the current professional literature, there are some indications that hoarding is a symptom of OCD. At times throughout this book, we will concur with the existing literature and agree that OCD may be related to hoarding for some people, but in other parts we will suggest that hoarding may exist independently of OCD since some people have hoarding symptoms without other symptoms of OCD.

People who engage in compulsive hoarding behaviors are typically called *hoarders*. A hoarder begins with an ordinary number of possessions, but as time goes on, the hoarder continues to purchase or collect more items, and the items begin to multiply and multiply and multiply. This continues until the person is living in chaos, often with their possessions in piles or stacks spread throughout their home and in extreme disarray.

The hoarder then reaches a boiling point and decides to throw everything away and start fresh, but has extreme difficulty in following through. The hoarder feels too overwhelmed to know where to start, or feels lost after trying for a while without seeing any visible progress. This results in a downward spiral that ends in frustration, depression, and hopelessness.

According to Karno and colleagues (1988), 2.5 percent of Americans suffer from OCD, which translates into approximately seven million people or roughly one out of every forty adults. One out of every two hundred kids suffers from OCD (Flament et al. 1988), and it does not discriminate across gender or race. For instance, in a typical elementary or middle school with one thousand students and one hundred and fifty teachers, administrators, and staff, approximately nine people will have OCD.

It has been much more difficult to accurately estimate the number of people suffering from hoarding. Researchers Frost and Steketee (1998) indicate that between one-quarter and one-third of those with OCD also have hoarding symptoms. The estimates we have may be on the low side, either because hoarders do not seek treatment or because they are too ashamed or embarrassed to mention their hoarding to their therapist. Furthermore, if hoarders do report their symptoms to therapists who are inexperienced in the treatment of hoarding, they typically drop out of treatment and become despondent.

What Is Hoarding?

Let's take a closer look at the symptoms of compulsive hoarding. We've already defined hoarding as acquiring and saving items that have little or no value and then having tremendous difficulty discarding them. The following list represents several other characteristics of hoarding. We will discuss each of them in more detail throughout the book.

Glance through these symptoms and see if any of them describe you or someone you know. Keep in mind that this is not a diagnostic tool, but just a list of the symptoms that we believe represent compulsive hoarding.

- avoids throwing away possessions
- has severe anxiety when attempting to discard possessions

- has trouble making decisions and cannot decide what to keep, where, and for how long

- has some level of subjective distress, including

   1. feeling overwhelmed or embarrassed by possessions

   2. feeling suspicious of others touching items

   3. depression

   4. anxiety

- has obsessive thoughts about possessions, including but not limited to

   1. fear of running out of an item

   2. fear of needing it later

   3. needing it "just in case"

   4. thoughts of checking the garbage to ensure an item was not accidentally discarded

- may have functional impairments, such as

   1. loss of space inside the home

   2. social isolation

   3. family or marital discord

   4. financial difficulties

   5. health hazards

- possessions are grossly disorganized

- has great difficulty categorizing items

Did you identify with any of the above symptoms? If you did, this book may be helpful to you. As you can see, hoarding can have a tremendous effect on people's lives and can disrupt every domain of functioning. Depression, anxiety, family tension, and divorce are common among hoarders and their family members.

This book is for people suffering from hoarding, and for their friends and families, whose lives have been torn apart by its effects. Our goal in this book is to help reduce or eliminate the shame that prevents people from getting treatment and to give a sense of hope that getting better is possible.

Life as a Hoarder

The stories of Bill and Gloria illustrate how hoarding is manifested differently in different people. Keep in mind that hoarding can affect people in a variety of ways, so don't stop reading or get discouraged if these examples are not exactly similar to your own hoarding behaviors.

Bill had recently retired from his job as an airline consultant, had been married for over twenty years, and was respected by his peers and clients. No one had ever questioned why Bill always preferred to meet clients or friends at restaurants instead of having them over for dinner. Nor did they ever think twice about why his daughter always went over to friends' houses rather than having playdates at home. There was always an excuse as to why the blinds were closed or why the windows were never opened.

Bill came to treatment reluctantly. His wife had told him that she would leave him unless he got treatment for his hoarding. He reported that his house was almost unbearable to live in anymore, but he felt too overwhelmed by the clutter to begin to make any changes. His previous attempts to clean up were unsuccessful, and he became very angry when others would try to help him throw things away.

Bill stated that if you looked hard enough in his living room, you could see the sofa, loveseat, and chair underneath the heaps of papers, plastic bags, and cardboard boxes that were stacked at eye level. Next to the sofa there was a snowblower and underneath the coffee table was a full-size car tire. He had desk drawers filled to capacity with rubber bands, batteries, and paper clips "just in case" he needed them in the future.

The kitchen was not very different. The six-person table was completely overrun by papers, plastic bags, and cardboard boxes. In fact, this was the only place in the entire house that could seat more than one person at a time. Family meals at the dinner table did not exist. Nor was there space for the family to retire to the living room and watch television together.

Bill discussed his extreme difficulty in discarding anything that was sent to the house. The previous year, he was able to cancel five of his fifteen magazine subscriptions, which cut down the number of magazines coming into the house. However, the remaining ten subscriptions, most of which came once a week for over seven years, had dominated both floor and countertop space, rendering the stovetop completely useless. The primary method of cooking was the microwave, but you had to step over boxes and crates to get there safely.

Bill had severe asthma and had no idea how much his symptoms had been exacerbated by the dirt, mold, and fungus that flourished in his house. Before Bill got treatment, he had not vacuumed or dusted anything in over four years. The shower stall in the bathroom had not been cleaned in years and was covered with a black mold that was very dangerous, as people invariably slipped on it. Following the treatment, his asthma was significantly better.

Gloria was a forty-year-old single mother of three children ranging in age from five to thirteen. She came to therapy for her fear of germs and diseases, a classic kind of OCD. She had a master's degree in special education, but because of the severity of her symptoms, she was able to work only a few days each month as a substitute teacher.

Gloria walked down the hallway of the office like a surgeon on her way to the operating room. Her elbows were out in front, her hands turned inward and just below eye level. Before sitting down, she pulled out one of the hundreds of antibacterial wipes from her purse and proceeded to cleanse the chair.

She stated that she washed her hands up to fifty times a day, often washing up to the elbow. Her fears of contamination started after the birth of her first daughter, when she was twenty-six years old. Prior to that, she did not recall any symptoms of OCD. She said that she knew her fears of getting sick were irrational but she felt compelled to wash and scrub anyway. Her biggest fear, however, was that her kids would learn from her hypervigilance about germs and live with the same amount of anxiety and fear as she did.

Gloria also had symptoms of compulsive hoarding. She reported that ever since she was a teenager, she'd had great difficulty throwing things away, especially paper products like newspapers, magazines, and mail (including junk mail). However, her hoarding behaviors were complicated by her fear of germs. She organized her clutter by the degree to which she felt the items had been contaminated from the outside world prior to entering the house.

When she came home from work or from doing errands, Gloria would evaluate the level of contamination she brought back to the house. Anything she considered "dirty" or contaminated with germs was wiped down with antibacterial wipes or paper towels before she felt comfortable putting it down inside. Once "decontaminated," the item was placed in a makeshift to-do pile. This pile was a vast area of clutter that spanned from the living room through the kitchen and into the dining room.

Although the clutter in the house was relatively under control, it did significantly interfere with Gloria's daily living. She had to-be-filed papers strewn across the living room floor, including important papers like tax returns and her kids' report cards. Other stacks domi-nated the sofa and chairs in the living room and could not be moved by anyone but Gloria, because if someone with dirty hands moved the papers, they would need decontamination again. It was if there were land mines in the living room and kitchen that had to be skill-fully maneuvered and traversed, and most often the kids would sit on the floor to do homework or watch television.

Gloria sometimes spent hours decontaminating possessions and would be exhausted afterward. At some point in every day, Gloria made a pact with herself that she would relieve her family of the mess and start to put things away. But every time she tried, she would start in one area and get sidetracked into another area, and then into another, until she became overwhelmed and frustrated. She eventually felt that it would be impossible for her to succeed and started to avoid the clutter altogether.

Exercise: Assess Yourself

Now that you have seen two different examples of how hoarding can affect people's lives, and you are becoming more familiar with compulsive hoarding, the next step is to evaluate your own symp-toms. Go through the following list of questions and answer them honestly. Remember, this book is designed to help you, so if you don't answer honestly, you're only cheating yourself.

This is not a diagnostic measurement. The answers you give will help you to understand yourself a little better.

Do you have difficulty throwing things away or get anxious when thinking about discarding your possessions?   Yes   No

Do you have so many possessions that your rooms are cluttered?
                                                       Yes   No

Do you often feel an urge to buy things or acquire free things, but know that you really don't need them?   Yes   No

Do you often decide to purchase or acquire items even if you know you have no space for them?   Yes   No

Do you have possessions taking up so much floor space that it is difficult to move around in the room?   Yes   No

Have you ever not been able to use a piece of furniture (a sofa, table, or chair) for its intended purpose because it was used as storage space for your possessions?   Yes   No

Have you ever been so embarrassed by the number of your possessions that you did not want people to see certain rooms in your house?   Yes   No

Has your saving or acquisition of possessions resulted in financial strain for you or your family?   Yes   No

Has the number of your possessions ever been the reason for arguments or disagreements within your family?   Yes   No

To what extent do your saving behaviors interfere with your functioning?   Not at all   Mildly   Moderately   Severely

How much time do you spend on tasks related to your saving behaviors each day, including thinking about your possessions? Less than 30 minutes/30 minutes to 2 hours/More than 2 hours

Do you often feel like you need additional storage space?
                                                                                    Yes   No

Have you actually required additional storage space?   Yes   No

Have your possessions ever been damaged because of inadequate storage space?   Yes   No

How much time each day do you spend looking for objects? Less than 30 minutes/30 minutes to 2 hours/More than 2 hours

Have you ever shoplifted as a way of acquiring possessions?
                                                                                    Yes   No

Have you ever been arrested for shoplifting?   Yes   No

How to Use This Book

This book is designed to help you understand compulsive hoarding. We encourage you to first skim through the book from beginning to end. This way you'll have a good overall grasp of hoarding. Then you should go through each chapter carefully, although you may find some chapters more helpful than others.

We also encourage you to keep a notebook and pen handy as you read on. We will ask you to write down your thoughts and feelings, and to complete other exercises like the self-assessment tool you just finished. You may wish to read the book along with a family member or friend if their support helps you feel more comfortable.

In order to overcome compulsive hoarding, it is important to understand every aspect of its nature. Chapter 1 will review the biological and sociological aspects of hoarding. We will also discuss one of the most commonly asked questions about hoarding: What is the difference between collectors and hoarders? Chapter 2 will discuss the reasons people hoard: fear, sentimentality, indecisiveness, and so on. Chapter 3 will review the damaging effects of hoarding on families, and will discuss legal issues that sometimes arise. Chapter 4 will discuss treatment options such as cognitive behavioral therapy and medications. We will also discuss motivational issues regarding treatment. Understanding the thoughts and emotions regarding hoarding are crucial to getting better. For this reason, chapter 5 will review cognitive therapy and how to apply these strategies in treatment. Chapters 6 and 7 will review the behavioral components to our treatment plan and will give specific techniques to help you get rid of clutter and make your home more functional. Finally, chapter 8 will discuss how to maintain the gains you have made in clearing the clutter and how to prevent relapses.

Although the task may seem overwhelming now, take heart: many other people have overcome compulsive hoarding, and you can too. We hope you are beginning to feel excited about freeing yourself from compulsive hoarding.

1

Understanding Compulsive Hoarding

The great thing in this world is not so much where we stand, as in what direction we are moving.

—Oliver Wendell Holmes Sr.

After reading through the diagnostic criteria for hoarding in the introduction, you may find yourself thinking that some of these symptoms could be representative of everyone, and could also apply to collectors. You may be unsure whether you are a hoarder or a collector. In this chapter we will differentiate between collecting and hoarding. We will then talk about some biological and sociological aspects of hoarding, as well as conditions that may exist along with hoarding.

Are You a Hoarder?

Let us start by clarifying who qualifies as a collector and who as a hoarder. Truthfully, almost every one of us has some characteristics of hoarding. Remember that just meeting one or two characteristics or criteria for a disorder or illness does not automatically mean that a person has the illness or disorder.

For example, a headache and a fever are two diagnostic criteria for a brain tumor. Does that mean that every time you have had a headache and a fever, you had a tumor? No! You can have a symptom without having the illness. Further, a headache and a fever are criteria for a host of illnesses including meningitis, encephalitis, strep throat, and the flu.

To be a hoarder, you need to fulfill a few of the criteria. The degree to which your symptoms interfere with your overall functioning is also a very important variable to consider. For instance, if you have some difficulty throwing away a week's worth of newspapers and they form a little pile on the floor, you probably are not a hoarder. But if you have six months' worth of newspapers scattered across the living room floor, making it difficult to get from one end of the room to the other, you may be a hoarder.

To be considered a hoarder, you need to have either a compulsion to save or difficulty discarding items you already possess, or both. The hoarding behavior causes distress to you or to others and interferes with your functioning. Even if you justify your hoarding behavior and you are not upset by it, you become upset if you cannot engage in the compulsion (that is, if you are prevented from keeping something you feel compelled to save, or if you have to throw away your possessions).

The Difference between Hoarding and Collecting

Hoarding is not the same as collecting. Generally speaking, collectors are proud of their possessions and enjoy showing them off. An avid car collector would enjoy driving his vintage sports car around the block; a boy who collects baseball cards would be proud to show them to his friends. Collectors often find joy in their collection and go out of their way to impress others. They make reference to their collection during conversations or go to conferences to meet others with similar interests. Collectors often have a specific location in their home for their collection. The child who collects baseball cards may have his cards in a special folder. Others may have their collection of stamps, cameras, figurines, or dishes laid out in a hutch or bookcase where viewing them is easy. Additionally, collectors budget and save their money to accommodate the purchase of new items and feel satisfied when adding them to the existing collection.

If you are a hoarder, however, you may be embarrassed by your possessions. You purchase items with the intention of finding some function for them but end up feeling embarrassed by them. When one item is purchased, another will follow, followed by another, and so on until there are more items than places to put them. This process usually results in clutter. Clutter is the product of either having too many items with not enough storage or feeling overwhelmed by the possessions and not knowing where to put them. Of course, you may hoard and not have clutter because you organize everything and put it away. However, most people who hoard do have clutter.

It is fairly common for hoarders to be so embarrassed by their possessions that they try to dissuade people from coming over to their homes. You may prefer to meet people at restaurants rather than having friends over for meals. This is the exact opposite of collectors. Hoarders prefer to purchase new appliances when the old ones break, because the thought of having repairmen at the house is too overwhelming. Steve, a hoarder for fifteen years, confessed that he did without a refrigerator for three years because he could not let anyone in his home to repair the one that broke, and he could not have a new one delivered because there was no space for it. As you can see, although there are a few overlapping qualities between hoarders and collectors, there are plenty of differences too.

Exercise: Are You a Collector or a Hoarder?

Here is a summary of the differences between hoarders and collectors. Check the boxes that you feel represent you. This is not a diagnostic tool. This is designed to help you understand the differences between hoarders and collectors. The more boxes you have checked in each category, the more likely you fall into that category.

Collectors

☐ feel proud of their possessions

☐ keep their possessions organized and well maintained

☐ find joy in their possessions and willingly display them to others

❑ attend meetings or conferences with others who share their interest

❑ enjoy conversations about their possessions

❑ budget their time and money around their possessions

❑ feel satisfaction when making additions to the collection

Hoarders

❑ feel embarrassed by their possessions

❑ have their possessions scattered randomly, often without any functional organization

❑ have clutter, often resulting in the loss of functional living space

❑ feel uncomfortable with others seeing their possessions, or outright refuse to let others view their possessions

❑ often have debt, sometimes extreme

❑ feel ashamed, sad, or depressed after acquiring additional items

---

If you checked off more boxes in the hoarder section, you may be a hoarder. The next section will help you identify what type of hoarder you are. This will help you to further understand your own hoarding behavior and allow you to target the problems better during the treatment stages. It is very important throughout this book to be honest with yourself. If you minimize or deny the problem, you will continue to suffer.

Types of Hoarding Behavior

A common misconception about hoarders is that they tend to acquire various unique and strange items. On the contrary, you may tend to acquire items that are the same that nonhoarders acquire, but in greater volume (Frost and Gross 1993). Possessions can come from compulsive buying or from compulsively seeking out free things. The possessions in the home of a nonhoarder may be identical to those in a hoarder's home, but the nonhoarder would have far fewer of them. Below is a list of the most commonly hoarded items. It is not a complete list, and your favorite items may not be listed.

newspapers or magazines	food or groceries
paper or plastic bags	mail
photographs	books
household supplies	toiletries
clothing or shoes	batteries
paper clips or rubber bands	pens
cardboard boxes	handouts or brochures
jewelry	tools

Compulsive Acquisition

Compulsive acquisition entails buying items impulsively and without much concern over spending money or accruing debt. If you are a hoarder who compulsively spends, you likely shop at wholesale stores in order to acquire greater numbers of items. It may be extremely difficult for you to pass up a bargain. Getting two for the price of one is a deal you may feel is too hard to resist.

Other ways of compulsively acquiring possessions include spending at retail sales and garage sales. Hoarders often spend full days going to garage sales in an effort to acquire great numbers of items. The idea that one person's garbage is another person's treasure rings true for hoarders. You may not be very selective in buying things and often leave garage sales with bags filled.

In the era of computers and the Internet, a new form of compulsive acquisition has been born. Maybe you have discovered Internet shopping, which allows you to never leave the confines of your home. Although sometimes viewed as a positive option, Internet shopping can be very dangerous and unhealthy for hoarders and those suffering from social anxiety disorder. Shopping from home may allow you to avoid long lines at the stores, the embarrassment of purchasing multiples of items, and spending excessive amounts of time away from home while trying to decide what to purchase. Although you may feel a sense of relief that you have avoided the uncomfortable feelings associated with shopping, Internet shopping tends to contribute to and maintain compulsive hoarding.

In some major metropolitan areas, there are services that deliver just about anything you can think of. For example, there are Internet sites in which you can do all your grocery shopping by picking out the products in Internet grocery stores. These stores allow you to walk down virtual aisles and pick out the very same groceries you could find at your local markets. Simply by clicking the mouse, you put the product in your "basket." You can pay online and have your groceries delivered to your house within a few hours. Other online stores will deliver rental movies, jewelry, even chewing gum: all you have to do is press a few buttons.

As you will learn in this book, the avoidance of feared or uncomfortable situations increases the fear of them later on. By shopping online and avoiding negative feelings, you may be shutting yourself off even further from the outside world and burying yourself deeper in the mountain of clutter and chaos.

Another form of compulsive acquisition is shoplifting. You may do this if you feel you need certain items but cannot afford them. Shoplifting is often difficult for hoarders to admit, and they are usually embarrassed or ashamed of it but have little control over it. Hoarders of this type may end up being banned from certain stores or arrested for shoplifting. They say it starts when they go on a shopping spree and then shoplift a few items because there is no way they can afford everything they feel compelled to buy.

Compulsively Getting Free Stuff

Generally speaking, written materials are the possessions most frequently acquired by hoarders. The majority of these items come from either retail or grocery stores. Often, in the entrance of a grocery store, there are racks of local newspapers and magazines with a sign above that states Free, Take One. Do you feel compelled to take one and find yourself taking many?

In fact, some hoarders don't need to read a sign in order to acquire free things. Sometimes, people will go through not only their own garbage cans but also through friends' and coworkers' garbage cans, or even Dumpsters, looking for items to take home.

Another easy way to acquire free things is simply to take things that are always available, such as professional cards, flyers, or other people's newspapers. When was the last time you went into a doctor's office and felt the urge to pick up pamphlets on various diseases, or appointment cards, or even a magazine here or there? Actually, there are many free things all around us. In the grocery store, you can pick up grocery bags, sample items, information about real estate, and many other things. Is it hard for you to pass up these freebies?

Seeking Perfect or Unique Items

Regardless of how they acquire their possessions, some hoarders look for perfect or unique items. Perfect or unique items are believed to have value because they are unlike others (Frost and Steketee 1998). For example, you may feel that if a handout has a typo, it is special because of its uniqueness. Further, if a handout has no typos and is in perfect condition, you may believe that it cannot be replaced. Anything can be presumed to be unique (for example, vases in unusual shapes, old containers, or badges); it is just a matter of the meaning you attach to the object. It does not really have to be unique. You may consider something precious and unique because it is the first one you have encountered, or because you believe it is rare even if it is not.

Just as you may find value in the uniqueness or perfection of an item, you may feel safe and secure with your possessions. The clutter that develops in your home may limit your ability to socialize and cause you to withdraw and spend more time at home with your possessions, in turn causing you to feel closer to your possessions. This spiral may lead you further away from your goal of changing your life.

Exercise: Identify Your Symptoms

This exercise is designed to help you understand your own hoarding symptoms. As you've learned, hoarding can affect people in very different ways, so it is important for you to understand how it affects you. Read through the following checklist and mark off the boxes you feel are representative of your hoarding, and when appropriate, list examples. Use your notebook if you need more space than is provided here. This exercise will come in handy when we discuss treatment issues, so be thorough with your answers.

❑ I have an excessive volume of possessions in my home.

❑ I compulsively acquire free things (go through garbage cans or Dumpsters, or collect flyers).

Examples: _____

❑ I compulsively buy or spend to acquire my possessions.

Examples: _____

❑ I am embarrassed by my possessions.

❑ I seek unique or perfect items.

Examples: _____

❑ I avoid throwing things away or feel very upset when throwing things away.

Examples: _____

❑ I have legal or financial troubles because of my hoarding.

Examples: _____

❑ I do not like to show other people my possessions.

Conditions Related to Compulsive Hoarding

Now that you have a better understanding of the behaviors associated with hoarding, let's see if you have a related disorder. Having a related disorder means that another disorder exists along with your hoarding. It is not necessarily the cause of your hoarding, but your hoarding behavior may be a symptom within that disorder.

So you need to determine whether you just have hoarding or have hoarding as a symptom within a different disorder. The disorders that are most often associated with hoarding are obsessive-compulsive personality disorder, OCD, and depression. The eating disorders, Prader-Willi syndrome, psychosis, and Alzheimer's disease are less frequently associated with hoarding. Pay attention to the symptoms of these disorders and see if you recognize yourself. Of course, you should have a professional evaluate you before you conclude that you have a particular disorder.

Obsessive-Compulsive Personality Disorder

The *Diagnostic and Statistical Manual, Fourth Edition (DSM-IV TR)* is the main diagnostic manual for mental health providers. It provides detailed clinical information on just about every mental disorder known. Within the *DSM-IV TR*, compulsive hoarding is listed only once as a symptom or diagnostic criteria for a disorder. That disorder is *obsessive-compulsive personality disorder* (OCPD), not to be confused with OCD, which we'll discuss later.

As with other types of personality disorders, OCPD can be misunderstood because of its name. It's not that people have a flaw or defect in their personality, or that a person is born with some sort of deficient personality. Rather, a person can have several characteristics, or personality traits, that can cause subjective distress, interfere with relationships, or be maladaptive in some way. Generally speaking, these personality traits are present beginning in early adulthood, are consistent across a variety of social and interpersonal situations, and are not related to reactions to drugs or medical conditions.

The *DSM-IV TR* characterizes OCPD as "a preoccupation with orderliness, perfectionism, and mental and interpersonal control, at the expense of flexibility, openness, and efficiency" (American Psychological Association 2000, 725). People with OCPD often pay close attention to details, lists, rules, and schedules, often to the extent that the major point of the activity is lost. They get so wrapped up in the details of how to do something that they forget why they're doing it.

Interestingly, although people with OCPD tend to be detail-oriented, they also tend to be indecisive. Indecisiveness is often the result of avoiding making a less-than-perfect decision. The person feels such intense discomfort with the potential of making a mistake that the decision is postponed or avoided altogether. We will discuss in chapter 2 how this results in the development and maintenance of clutter.

Exercise: Do You Have OCPD?

If you have identified with the above description, you may suffer from OCPD. The following chart represents all the diagnostic criteria for OCPD. Mark the traits that you feel you have. If you check four or more of them, you may suffer from OCPD. Keep in mind that a diagnosis can only be made by a qualified therapist and the following criteria are given solely to help you gain insight into your own behaviors.

❑ I am preoccupied with details, rules, lists, order, organization, or schedules to the extent that the major point of the activity is lost.

❑ I am excessively devoted to work and productivity to the exclusion of leisure activities and friendships (not accounted for by obvious economic necessity).

❑ I am unable to discard worn-out or worthless objects even when they have no sentimental value.

❑ I adopt a miserly spending style toward myself and others; money is something to be hoarded for future catastrophes.

❑ I show perfectionism that interferes with task completion (for example, I am unable to complete a project because my own overly strict standards are not met).

❑ I am overconscientious, scrupulous, and inflexible about matters of morality, ethics, or values (not accounted for by cultural or religious identification).

❑ I am reluctant to delegate tasks or to work with others unless they submit to exactly my way of doing things.

❑ I am rigid and stubborn.

Obsessive-Compulsive Disorder

Although hoarding is not listed in the *DSM-IV TR* as a diagnostic criterion, hoarding is generally associated with OCD. OCD consists of three major symptoms: obsessions, compulsions, and doubting. *Obsessions* are intrusive, forceful, and useless thoughts or images that become stuck in one's mind and cannot be suppressed. Obsessions interfere greatly with everyday thinking and cause anxiety and sometimes depression. Commonly reported obsessions include the fear of harming oneself or others, fearing contamination, aggressive or sexual thoughts, thoughts of symmetry, and mentally reviewing conversations. If you are a hoarder, you may have obsessions about your possessions or where you placed something because you fear losing it. In this way, obsessions may be a part of your life.

Compulsions are the actions or mental behaviors that one feels a strong need to perform, usually in response to an obsession, in order to reduce anxiety. Common compulsions include washing, checking, repeating or retracing, touching, ordering and arranging, and praying. When people experience obsessions and compulsions, they recognize their thoughts and behaviors as excessive or unreasonable, but have great difficulty in ignoring or suppressing them, and they continue over and over for minutes, hours, and even days. Hoarders may manifest compulsions by compulsively acquiring new objects.

Doubt is one of the core features of OCD and is present in almost every obsession. For example, people with OCD may have an obsession that because they shook hands with another person, they have germs on their hands and will get sick unless they wash (washing in this case is the compulsion). They are not certain about this thought and doubt that they will indeed get sick. However, they do not want to take any risks. While driving, some people with OCD frequently fear that they have hit someone in the road and feel the overwhelming need to go back and check. You may identify with the symptom of doubting if you cannot decide what to do with a particular possession.

As you can see, although their names share the words *obsessive-compulsive*, OCD and OCPD are very different disorders. In fact, society and the media often confuse them. Various Hollywood movies and television shows often depict characters as being highly focused on details or rules. We either are told that they have OCD or, from ignorance, we assume they do. In fact, they probably have OCPD.

For the purposes of gaining insight into your own feelings and behaviors, you must be clear about the differences between OCD and OCPD. The person with OCD generally wants to get rid of the obsessions and compulsions that produce anxiety. This is very different from people with OCPD, who usually do not mind their way of being and usually take pride in their behaviors. They generally do not experience distress, and if they seek help, it is usually because they have difficulty getting along with others. People with OCPD generally do not have obsessions or compulsions as we have defined them here. They tend to firmly believe their thoughts or positions about things and go out of their way to follow them.

OCD versus OCPD

A person with OCD	A person with OCPD
• has obsessions (unwanted, repetitive, and intrusive thoughts that cause extreme anxiety)	• is perfectionistic, rule oriented, and inflexible
• engages in compulsions (washing, repeating, checking, etc.) to ease the anxiety from obsessions	• has a stubborn and rigid personality style
• knows that symptoms are problematic and may have insight regarding the irrationality of symptoms	• generally is not personally bothered by symptoms, despite their interference in interpersonal relationships

You may be wondering how OCD and hoarding are related. Most of the research suggests that hoarding is a symptom of OCD, yet only 25 to 35 percent of individuals with OCD actually hoard (Frost and Steketee 1998). It is associated with OCD mostly because hoarders have obsessions about their possessions, compulsions to hoard, and doubt about what to discard. Hoarders may think a lot about their possessions. They may wonder where something was placed, whether something was accidentally thrown out, whether someone touched their belongings, or how to organize their possessions. They may find it hard to resist the urge to save and to not discard. Throwing things out causes great distress, and they avoid the distress by hoarding. Hoarding is a compulsion that reduces the uncomfortable feelings, and thus is a form of OCD.

Depression

When we become depressed, our interest and motivation to accomplish things often takes a backseat to our mood. We tend to spend more time in bed and less time doing exercise; we eat more (or fewer) calories than usual and have feelings of worthlessness and guilt. For many people, hoarders and nonhoarders alike, this is when clutter develops and builds.

When you're depressed, sometimes you are less motivated to follow through with your everyday responsibilities. You may postpone important tasks or procrastinate and avoid your responsibilities. Letting bills pile up, not getting around to returning phone calls, leaving a sinkful of dishes, and letting your home become more dirty or cluttered than usual are just some of the ways depression can influence your daily life.

Other times, in an attempt to lift your depression, you may purchase new things for yourself. You may think that perhaps a new pair of shoes will improve your mood, or a few new CDs will help lift your spirits. But if clutter has developed, chances are the new possessions will just join the others and get lost in the clutter, and you will never get the opportunity to try them out. You may then feel guilty or regretful about wasting the money or not having enough discipline to organize the possessions and enjoy them.

The interaction between hoarding and depression can be quite powerful and, at times, damaging. As clutter or chaos builds, our emotions follow suit. As our lives and homes become more chaotic, the very sight of the clutter may trigger thoughts of low self-worth, hopelessness, or the feeling of being overwhelmed. This downward spiral into depression and negative self-evaluation decreases the motivation for change.

Hoarding, OCD, and OCPD are often accompanied by depression. If you think about it, it makes sense. All the disorders can cause significant anxiety, discomfort, and frustration, which may result in social isolation, sadness, and decreased enjoyment in life. Additionally, depression can influence the severity and frequency of symptoms in all three disorders.

Depression and hoarding share some qualities, and it's sometimes difficult to figure out which came first, the hoarding or the depression. Sometimes hoarding is the result of depression, and sometimes depression is a result of hoarding. In either case, hoarding can have a tremendous influence on a person's confidence and mood.

We mentioned earlier that common behaviors in compulsive hoarding tend to isolate hoarders from others in their lives, often the people closest to them: family and friends. Think about your own life. How has hoarding isolated you from others? Very often, hoarders are too embarrassed by their clutter to allow friends and even family members to enter the house. Sometimes the amount of clutter in a room renders the room useless. Coffee tables, sofas, chairs, and floor spaces are used for storage rather than for their intended functions. The less functional the rooms become, the more you become isolated from others, and the more likely you will feel depressed.

In this case, the hoarder feels what we call *secondary depression*. If you magically took away the hoarding, the depression would disappear as well. The hoarding is causing the depression. We'll discuss this in more detail in the chapters dedicated to treatment approaches.

Conditions Less Frequently Associated with Hoarding

Psychosis, dementia, eating disorders, pica, and Prader-Willi syndrome are disorders in which hoarding behaviors have sometimes been observed, but these conditions are much less common than OCPD, OCD, and depression. Acknowledging and treating the hoarding in these conditions may help to alleviate some distress within the condition.

Psychosis

According to the *DSM-IV TR,* the *psychotic disorders* are a group of nine conditions that have in common the presence of hallucinations, delusions, or both; disorganization of thought; drastic changes in mood; and poor insight about one's condition. *Schizophrenia* is the most common of the psychotic disorders, and hoarding is sometimes associated with it.

Schizophrenia is a condition whereby a person has hallucinations, delusions, or both. A *hallucination* is a perceptual disturbance in which a person sees, hears, smells, tastes, or feels something that is not actually there. A *delusion* is a strong belief that is either a distortion of reality or grossly untrue. These symptoms may be accompanied by social isolation, depression, and poor social skills.

Some people with schizophrenia have *paraphernalia,* meaning that they collect and store useless objects. Paraphernalia was very common in psychiatric hospitals until the advent of medications for psychosis in the 1950s. For example, James was a forty-two-year-old man with psychosis who collected literally hundreds of yards of aluminum foil. He lined every wall in his house with the foil because he believed it protected him from the radiation waves he thought were penetrating his home.

Dementia

Dementia is a progressive and deteriorative condition that causes marked differences in almost every domain of human functioning. These changes in functioning affect personality, memory, thought processes, judgment, motivation, intellectual ability, and insight. There are actual anatomical changes that occur in the brain as the dementia progresses.

As a society, we are becoming more familiar with a certain type of dementia, *Alzheimer's disease.* Because celebrities such as Ronald Reagan and Charlton Heston announced publicly their battles with Alzheimer's disease, we are becoming more aware of its damaging effects. However, people are not yet as familiar with hoarding as an aspect of Alzheimer's.

In fact, hoarding is often seen in Alzheimer's disease. When you walk into the house of someone with Alzheimer's, you notice possessions all over the place without order or organization. Objects accumulate on shelves, counters, tables, and floors. People with Alzheimer's commonly save newspapers, magazines, mail, and envelopes, or nostalgic items (photographs, clothing, and memorabilia). Poor judgment, loss of organizational skills, erratic or absent memory, and repetitive behaviors can often exacerbate this collecting and saving.

Diogenes' syndrome is another form of dementia in which hoarding is observed. This syndrome is characterized by self-neglect, squalor, and hoarding. Many people with Diogenes' syndrome live alone or are widowed, have isolated themselves socially, and have grossly dirty and unorganized homes with no sense of shame or embarrassment. They also appear disheveled and dirty, and tend to have multiple physical complications (Williams et al. 1998).

Eating Disorders

There are three major eating disorders: primary anorexia nervosa, bulimia nervosa, and compulsive overeating. These conditions are associated with OCD because they involve obsessive and compulsive symptoms. Hoarding has been indirectly linked to eating disorders because of the saving behavior observed in these disorders, primarily the hoarding of food. Remember, although there is a link between the eating disorders and hoarding, it certainly does not mean that all hoarders have eating disorders or that all those with eating disorders hoard.

Anorexia nervosa is a refusal to maintain body weight at or above a minimally normal weight. People with anorexia generally tend to starve themselves, which in turn may lead them to hoard food as well as other objects like glass or cardboard boxes. Although anorexics sometimes hoard food, they usually do not eat the saved items.

Bulimia nervosa is defined as recurrent episodes of binge eating. Bulimics consume a large amount of food within a very short period of time, and bingeing is sometimes followed by *purging* (self-induced vomiting). These episodes are characterized by lack of control over eating. Bulimics tend to gather large quantities of food and in that way mimic hoarding.

Compulsive eating, in contrast, is the consumption of large amounts of food over an extended period of time. Eventually, the individual can no longer lose weight and may become morbidly obese. Compulsive overeaters tend to hoard food and hide it from family members. They are secretive about the hoarding behavior, and once discovered, they experience feelings of guilt and shame.

Pica

Related to the eating disorders is a condition known as *pica*. Pica is the impulsive eating of inedible things such as paper, clay, paint chips, hair, clothes, or toothpaste. Pica is named for the Latin word for "magpie," a bird noted for eating nonnutritive objects or carrying them away.

Prader-Willi Syndrome

Prader-Willi syndrome is a genetic condition characterized by insatiable eating, self-mutilation, and limited intellectual capability. People with Prader-Willi syndrome can't tell when they are full and therefore keep eating indefinitely. They hoard food in their pocketbook or under their bed in order to eat it later when no one is looking.

The More You Know, the Better Off You'll Be

As you can see, hoarding can be part of a variety of different psychiatric and medical conditions. We hope this chapter has given you a better understanding of your own hoarding behaviors and the condition or conditions related to it. Although most people have hoarding alone, or hoarding associated with depression, OCD, or OCPD, it is important to understand all the clinical manifestations of hoarding. In fact, understanding the connection between your hoarding and a clinical disorder may be an important factor in your recovery.

The Biological and Sociological Aspects of Hoarding

In addition, understanding the biological and sociological aspects of hoarding will further increase your insight. Let us now explore some explanations of hoarding from a biological and sociological perspective.

Biological Aspects of Hoarding

The brain is the organ that rules our body, which makes us dependent on it. Certainly, every part of our life needs to go through the filter of our body, which includes our brain. Hoarding is no exception. In fact, every animal uses its brain to connect it to the surrounding world.

To have an idea of how the brain works, think of the *neuron,* the smallest unit of functioning within the brain. In the giant squid, a single neuron provides the squid with the capacity to function. This makes the giant squid one of the simplest organisms in the world.

The human brain, however, consists of literally billions of neurons. Each neuron is interconnected with thousands of other neurons. This gigantic net of neurons allows the human brain to function. All these neurons establish their connections by means of biochemical messengers known as *neurotransmitters.* Messages received or transmitted by the brain follow pathways traveled by neurotransmitters. The neurotransmitters carry the information to different parts of the brain.

There are five *lobes* or segments of our brain, and each lobe is responsible for a different general aspect of functioning. However, it is the interaction between lobes that is responsible for more-specific aspects of functioning. All the lobes are united through several million neurons that carry information. The neurons are able to establish loops or circuits between areas, and these loops often involve their own chemistry. Therefore, a combination of anatomy and chemistry is required to carry messages from the outside world into the body and vice versa.

One circuit of interest is the *cortico-striato-thalamo-cortical circuit,* which represents one of the anatomical models of OCD. It is possible that this circuit may be involved with hoarding as well. This loop operates with its own neurotransmitter chemistry.

There are two major neurotransmitters that are involved in the study of the biological explanation of hoarding, dopamine and serotonin. *Dopamine* is responsible for regulating our motor movements, emotions, and moods. *Serotonin* is an important neurotransmitter apparently associated to OCD and related disorders. Therefore, we may infer that serotonin and dopamine may influence the mechanism of hoarding.

In tiny amounts, serotonin exerts a powerful influence in the mechanisms of behaviors and mood regulation. In order to break down serotonin into its byproducts, vitamin B_6 is required. A faulty serotonin mechanism may contribute to OCD and its related disorders. Interestingly, a deficiency in vitamin B_6 causes rats to hoard (Gross and Cohn 1954).

Can we conclude that a surplus or deficit of these major neurotransmitters causes hoarding? There is no direct evidence that supports this hypothesis, but we do know that dopamine and serotonin are very important in the mechanism of OCD. We certainly know that within OCD there are many cases of hoarding, which further reinforces this hypothesis. It is possible that the correlation between OCD and hoarding indicates there are chemical similarities as well. This is an area of research that needs more work.

Fear Mechanisms in Hoarding

Fear is a basic emotion that protects the human and animal body from danger. The presence of fear warns the body of the possibility of harm or death. This state of alarm requires the body to defend itself by creating a system of protection from harmful events and predators. Our bodies protect us by seeking food, shelter, energy, and clothing. Without these elements, humans would perish.

Modern humans living in technologically advanced societies take these protections for granted and readily assume they will be provided to us. Modern societies are focused on gathering money or objects that protect us only indirectly and serve to enhance our self-image. Ownership of property now reflects what was once believed to be of utmost importance: food ownership. We feel powerful and capable of protecting our integrity by owning possessions.

This urge to acquire is exaggerated in people who hoard. Their attitude and behavior may go unnoticed by those who live with them, until the hoarder has collected so much clutter that the hoarding cannot be concealed. The idea of hoarding as a response to fear may help explain the biological underpinnings of the hoarder's reality.

We know that both humans and animals tends to hoard food and other items when they are starving (Keys et al. 1950; Cabanac and Swiergiel 1989). Interestingly, they do not necessarily eat the food that they hoard. We'll talk more in the next chapter about how fear—and specifically the primal fear of starvation—relates to hoarding in people who aren't under conditions of starvation.

A Sociological Look at Hoarding

One problem we all have is that we tend to equate *having* with *being.* This takes us back almost to the beginning of humankind, when we started to find our place among so many animals, not yet knowing our role on this planet. From our origins, humans have striven to achieve happiness through acquiring possessions. Many great philosophers, including Buddha, Moses, Jesus, Mohammed, Meister Eckhart, and Marx, tell us that it is only in *being* that we will achieve happiness.

Our Society Influences Who We Think We Are

We live in a modern, technologically advanced era when it is not uncommon to hear that he who dies with the most toys wins. We have come to believe that material possessions define who we are and that our self-worth is directly connected to the quantity and quality of our possessions. Yet as much as we try to convince ourselves that possessions define us, often we can't wait to get away from them. We go on vacations in order to live a more simple life and just be. Ironic, isn't it, that we spend so much time, energy, and money acquiring possessions, but we find so much peace away from them.

When was the last time you saw a commercial on television that said something like *You have so many good qualities and characteristics, you don't need to buy our product* or *You don't need our product to be cool, you're cool already*? Almost every form of advertising is designed to have you believe that you would be a little better off if you owned the products they are selling.

Our society emphasizes acquiring and having possessions. We live in a society that marks national holidays as an opportunity to sell us more possessions. For example, do you spend Martin Luther King Jr. Day, Presidents' Day, or Memorial Day actually observing those people or events, or do you find yourself at retail shops for the big holiday sales? We often have spring-cleaning modes when we are encouraged to get rid of the old and bring in the new possessions. We are encouraged to discard clothing that is no longer in style and purchase new lines of clothing that designers determine are trendy. But it seems that every time we discard an "old" style, eventually society tells us it has made a comeback, and we are encouraged to acquire it again.

Now, we don't want to give the impression we are antimedia or paranoid, but it is important to understand from a psychosocial perspective how our society persuades us to acquire and own, rather than just be. Hoarders tend to confuse society's message of *Out with the old, in with the new* and get stuck on a need to possess. While nonhoarders are doing their spring-cleaning, you may find yourself trying to acquire more and more, while keeping the old. Although this may fulfill a desire or need, it inevitably causes problems, primarily in the form of clutter.

Many of the people who have come to us for treatment have experienced a multitude of interpersonal, marital, and even legal problems. As clutter builds in the home of a hoarder, pathways need to be made so that people can get through each room without hurting themselves. This often becomes a danger not only for the hoarder but also for their family members, especially children.

Unfortunately, we have seen many hoarders who were going through bitter divorce and child custody proceedings because their spouses reported them to state housing departments or child welfare agencies. Hoarders can face many difficult and stressful legal issues due to blocked fire escapes, lack of routine meter inspections, failure to arrange for the repair of appliances, and the inability to provide a safe and clean environment for children.

Many states are setting up task forces to help hoarders with their problems so that they can prevent evictions and legal problems. It is fairly common for state child welfare agencies to take children out of homes that have dangerous amounts of clutter. Other state agencies, usually through their housing departments, can mandate that demolition or excavation crews take action to enforce regulations without the consent of the homeowner. We have seen people whose possessions had been thrown into Dumpsters and containers brought in by state agencies and who were later evicted from the premises.

As you can see, compulsive hoarding involves much more than simply acquiring and failing to discard possessions. It can also involve interpersonal conflict, marital distress, personal stress, depression, and legal problems. We will discuss these sociological issues in greater detail in chapter 3.

We hope this book will help you understand your own hoarding behaviors and give you a healthy means to prevent some of these devastating issues from affecting your life.

2

Why Do You Save?

You can't have everything, where would you put it?

—Steven Wright

As you saw in the last chapter, people exhibit hoarding behaviors across a variety of different psychological and medical conditions, and we have explained the methods they use to acquire their possessions. This chapter will discuss the various reasons why people save the items they've acquired. Understanding your own personal reasons for your saving is crucial in order to change your behaviors later. Further, we often use different treatment approaches for different kinds of acquiring and saving behaviors.

It is interesting that although hoarding symptoms can occur within so many psychological conditions, the reasons why people feel the need to acquire and save possessions are often quite different. You may acquire and save the exact same type of item as someone else, but for very different reasons.

For example, paycheck stubs are an item commonly saved by compulsive hoarders. We have seen people who saved literally decades' worth of paycheck stubs. Some people saved them in case they were audited or needed them in the future. Others, however, saved them because the stubs were trophies in a sense, representing tasks they had accomplished and showing they had been success-fully employed. This is just one example of how two people with apparently similar saving patterns can actually be saving for very different reasons. In fact, it is impossible to have two identical cases of compulsive hoarding.

Exercise: Identify the Reasons Why You Save

Before you read further, take out the notebook you have been using along with this book. Write down as many reasons as you can think of for saving your possessions. To help you out, we have listed ten of the most common reasons. This list is certainly not exhaustive of the reasons why people save things, and the list is in no particular order of importance. We will discuss these reasons (and others) as we progress through the book.

- You keep it "just in case" a need for it arises in the future.

- You feel that if it's unique, it can't be replaced.

- You feel that you can give the item a good home or protect it from outside influences.

- You can't decide exactly where it should go, so you just hold on to it.

- You believe that you will feel horrible later if you make a mistake by throwing it away now.

- If it has even the slightest bit of value, you can't throw it away.

- You can't remember why you saved it in the first place, but you must have had your reasons, so you keep it.

- You can't throw away printed information until you read it, understand it, or remember it.

- It has sentimental value to you.

- Although it isn't valuable now, it may become valuable in the future.

So What Are You Afraid Of?

Although people save for different reasons, we believe that fear is the basic reason behind the drive to save. Fear is the foundation and basis of many human behaviors. If you think about the bare essentials for human survival, food and shelter are crucial. If you were magically transported to a distant, uninhabited tropical island, you might at first feel relieved to be away from the demands of everyday life. But once you figured out that no one was coming to get you and you were stranded, you would feel afraid and scared. Your first instinct would be to find shelter and food. This is called *self-preservation*, because you would want to survive.

We believe that over time, your core human fear of being without food and shelter may have overlapped with your feelings toward your possessions. This association then caused you to feel fearful and unsafe when you were without possessions. We believe that you may have learned to temporarily avoid feeling fear by feeling secure and safe with your possessions.

Because humans are creatures of habit, the more you were able to avoid fear and feel safe by acquiring or saving possessions, the stronger your need to acquire or save became over time. Often, the quantity of items influences this feeling, so the more items you have, the safer you feel. So in a sense, your hoarding behaviors were conditioned by your fear of not having shelter and food, and they have been maintained by your continual acquisition or saving of items. In other words, without your possessions you feel fearful or unsafe, and in order to avoid those unpleasant feelings you don't discard any of your possessions.

Deprivation Leads to Desperation

When you consider the sense of safety your possessions give you and the belief that without possessions you are weak or lost, it makes sense that if friends or family discarded items without your consent, you would be very hurt or angry. Your sense of safety is threatened and you feel frightened. Your self-preservation is taken away.

Think about it this way: What would happen if you tried to take away a bowl of food from a starving dog? The dog would probably bark or snap with anger and try to bite you. The dog may not really want to hurt you, but its survival instinct to defend its food causes an involuntary angry reaction.

That is similar to what happens when family members or friends try to clean clutter without your consent. We hope you haven't actually barked or tried to bite anyone, but you probably felt very angry or hurt.

The feeling of loss when others discard items without your consent can be incredibly difficult to bear. Some hoarders say they think about their possessions while working or out with friends, and feel great comfort and relief when they go home and see their possessions. Hoarders often feel violated when their families go behind their back and discard items without their knowing.

Perhaps you fear that feeling of loss so much that you refuse to leave your possessions alone with others or check garbage cans for items that could have been discarded. This gives you a greater sense of control, not only over your possessions but also over your environment. Has this ever happened to you? Have you ever experienced these feelings?

Ironically, although you may feel safe with your possessions and feel as if you have greater control over your environment, you're probably at the same time feeling tremendous embarrassment and shame about the clutter. The perceived control and safety that you have comes at the expense of functional living space and true happiness. Bear in mind that as human beings we not only have basic instincts of self-preservation, but also develop beliefs, values, and feelings around our behaviors. We attach meaning to objects, and we learn to think and feel certain emotions in certain situations. Imagine being without your possessions. Would you feel uncomfortable, unprotected, unsafe, insecure, and all alone out there in life?

Exercise: Identify Your Feelings about Your Possessions

This is an important exercise. Your answers will come in very handy later, when you are looking at how to change the way you feel. Before you can change your feelings, you need to identify your thoughts and beliefs.

Take out your notebook and rewrite the following sentences on a new page. After you copy the sentences, fill in the blanks about how you feel in each of the situations. Write down as many feelings as you can for each blank.

I feel _____ when my possessions are discarded without my consent.

When I'm away from my possessions, I feel _____ .

When I'm near my possessions, I feel _____ .

I feel _____ when my family and friends talk about my hoarding.

I wish I could _____ in the future.

When people comment about the clutter, I feel _____ .

If strangers see my clutter, I feel _____ .

I feel _____ when I make a mistake.

What's Your Saving Pattern?

There are a few types of saving patterns that may explain why you hoard. Keep in mind that it is the volume of the saved items—not the actual items—that differentiates you from someone who does not hoard. Remember that everyone is different; some people may incorporate all these patterns, and others may have none.

Sentimental Saving

Sentimental saving (Furby 1978) happens when a person attaches an emotion to a possession, then associates that item with the emotion. For example, a person might look at an empty matchbook and remember that he picked up that matchbook while having a nice dinner out with his family. He then associates that happy memory with the matchbook and thinks that if he throws it away, he will be throwing away part of a fond memory, so he decides to save it. Certainly, if you keep taking matchbooks from restaurants and deciding to keep them because they serve as reminders of positive experiences, then before you know it, you will have piles and piles of them. Of course, you could also attach negative feelings to items, although this is not as common.

Instrumental Saving

Instrumental saving (Furby 1978) occurs when a person feels that an item must be saved because it could be used in the future. This is where the just-in-case reasoning is applied. A woman might find a pair of shoes in her closet that she hasn't worn in over two years but decide to keep them "just in case" she needs them in the future. Or you might keep desk drawers filled with rubber bands, paper clips, and pencils "just in case" you need them in the future.

Hoarders tend to overestimate the probability of needing items, and at the same time underestimate their ability to cope with not having enough supplies. This type of saving is not limited to hoarders, however. Everyone can relate to this in times of severe weather. Newscasters usually give reports and updates outside local hardware and grocery stores recommending that people hurry down to the stores and stock up on supplies in case the impending storm knocks out power lines or causes driving hazards. Some hoarders live that scenario all the time; they are always looking for ways to prepare for future catastrophes or times of need. This is where fear comes into play again. The just-in-case reasoning helps keep the person from feeling unsafe or unprotected.

Saving for Aesthetic Value

Saving items because they have some sort of aesthetic value is less common than the other two types of saving. We worked with a woman who liked to save "junk art," which was usually welded pieces of metal that just "looked cool" to her. You may like the way something appears in color, texture, shape, or size and save it based on those characteristics. Once again, the saving behavior becomes a problem because it is not just one item but many, and clutter develops.

Exercise: Identify Your Saving Style

In your notebook, make a simple chart by writing the words *Sentimental*, *Instrumental*, and *Aesthetic* on the same horizontal line but spaced apart. After each word, draw a vertical line down to the bottom of the page. Underneath each category, list as many possessions as you can think of, and next to each possession, write down why it falls in that category.

For example, let us assume you save newspapers. Write down *newspapers* under the category that best explains why you save them. Note that you may put items in more than one category. For instance, do you save the newspapers because they remind you of important events (sentimental), or because you are afraid you might need the information in the future (instrumental), or because you are fascinated by the pictures (aesthetic). Go through this process with as many possessions as you can.

Common Traits of Hoarders

Although there are three categories for saving behaviors, there are a host of traits or characteristics you may have that can contribute to and maintain your hoarding behaviors. You may identify with one or several or all of the following characteristics. Keep in mind that the number of traits that you identify with (or don't identify with) does not in any way indicate the severity of your hoarding. If you can relate to all of these, you are not necessarily suffering from more severe hoarding than someone who identifies with only one or two.

Fear of Losing Information

Hoarders often believe that discarding a possession, generally a ~~newspaper or magazine~~, means they are throwing away information. This type of saving we refer to as the fear of losing information.

This type can seem similar to instrumental saving. The difference is that we are talking more about *information* one may need in the future than about some item or object. One of the high expectations that hoarders often set for themselves is that they cannot discard written information until they have read it and understood it. The just-in-case reasoning is often applied to this as well.

We have worked with several hoarders who believed that there was a need to know specific information in the future, so they held on to literally hundreds of unread newspapers. Clutter developed because newspapers and magazines entered their homes much faster than they could read them. One man stored newspapers under his bed until the papers literally lifted the bed off the floor. Another patient's husband complained he was unable to entertain for business purposes because his wife's newspapers were scattered from the front door of their house all the way to their basement.

Indecisiveness

When conducting clinical interviews, we sometimes chuckle to ourselves when asking people if they are indecisive. If someone replies, "Yes, I'm indecisive," then they are responding decisively about being indecisive.

But seriously, many hoarders are indecisive (Warren and Ostrom 1998). They may be indecisive about what clothes to wear, what to order at restaurants, what movies to see, and so on. Certainly, they are indecisive about their possessions. Think about whether you are an indecisive person. What are you indecisive about? Are you indecisive just about what to discard, but pretty certain about other decisions you have to make?

You may openly admit to being indecisive about your possessions. You probably begin to feel anxious or uncomfortable at the thought of having to decide what to discard. You may procrastinate day after day because making a decision makes you feel uneasy, anxious, and perhaps fearful. By not making the decision, you are able to escape those unpleasant emotions and feel secure again. You may be able to deal with postponing the decision by saying something to the effect of *I'll figure it out later.*

Perhaps you acquire something new and are unsure where to put it. Afraid of putting it in the wrong spot, you avoid making that decision and opt to "just put it here for now." Again, in order to avoid the unpleasant emotions that accompany making a mistake, you see postponing the decision as a viable option. But that later time never comes, so you never decide where to put the new item, and the end product is clutter. The more this happens, the more likely you will delay other decisions, leading to more clutter and disorganization.

Keep in mind that more is lost with indecision than with bad decision. Ask yourself which of these options is healthier for you: living in a disorganized, cluttered house because you avoided feeling negative emotions, or temporarily feeling uncomfortable but living in a home where you can use the furniture and walk around freely without stepping on your possessions.

In a sense, you have chosen to live in clutter and disorganization by deceiving yourself into thinking that you are unable to make decisions and feel uncomfortable. Do you tend to make decisions easily, or is it sometimes painful to make decisions? Do you avoid doing certain things to avoid feeling uncomfortable? Write down in your notebook a few things that you usually have trouble making decisions about and what emotions you feel when attempting to make a decision.

Fear of Making a Mistake

Warren and Ostrom (1988) suggest that hoarders tend to fear making mistakes. Mistakes that hoarders tend to worry about making commonly include

- not being prepared for the future

- misplacing possessions

- throwing something away accidentally

- not finding the "perfect" place for a possession

If you are afraid of making the mistake of not being prepared for the future, you may buy many similar items. Before you know it, there are multiples of everything you purchased and not enough room for any of them.

Another common mistake hoarders fear making is misplacing items. This is why many hoarders have all their items in plain sight. Are you afraid if you put something away you may not be able to find it later, or worse, you may even forget about it? The fear of forgetting about an item is quite common. Unfortunately, because of the volume of your possessions, you probably don't remember why you saved the particular item in the first place.

Perhaps you are fearful of making a mistake about where to place something. Does it take you a long time to decide where to place an item because you don't want to make a wrong decision? Another common belief is that if you accidentally throw something out without examining it well, you may regret it later, or that when something gets thrown out, there may have been another item of value attached to it.

Indecisiveness + Fear of Making a Mistake = Clutter

As you can imagine, being either indecisive or fearful of making a mistake can cause significant distress and impairment of functioning within a life. Combine the two, however, and you have a recipe for clutter. As it turns out, many hoarders are both indecisive and fearful of making mistakes, which helps explain the world of delayed decision making, avoidance of feeling, and clutter in which they live.

Inability to Prioritize

The combination of indecisiveness, fear of making mistakes, and the volume of items often makes it difficult for hoarders to prioritize tasks. For example, we worked with a young man who wanted desperately to get household chores completed during his weekends. However, because he felt that each of the tasks (putting up venetian blinds, painting walls, moving furniture) was equally important, he was not able to figure out which to do first. Because of his indecisiveness and fear of making mistakes, he felt very uncomfortable having to decide which task to do first. So he avoided making any decisions and spent his weekends alone and depressed in his unfinished house.

This type of situation occurs with many hoarders. Do you have difficulty prioritizing things in your life? Do you walk from one pile of clutter to another, not really sure where to start? If you do, then you probably feel overwhelmed by the task of cleaning up.

For many hoarders, difficulty prioritizing leads to procrastination. You may tell yourself that somehow your decision will be clearer later. Unfortunately, the decision is not easier later. In fact, it is probably more difficult later because you feel ashamed that you could not figure it out earlier. Additionally, you may also have more piles of clutter surrounding you later, which only compounds your negative emotions.

Fear of Loss

Some people have a disproportionate fear of accidentally discarding an important item. They decide it's better to be safe than sorry, and keep the item "just in case."

It is very common for hoarders to closely inspect items before throwing them away in order to avoid losing something valuable. For example, as you prepare to throw out your magazines, you may feel the need to go through them page by page to make sure something of value (like a check or an important phone number) is not accidentally thrown out.

Unfortunately, sometimes this does happen. A very common phenomenon within hoarding is what Frost and Steketee (1998) call *churning*. Churning happens when you attempt to clean one pile and instead mix the contents of that pile in with another. So you end up with two intermixed piles rather than one organized space.

A problem with churning is that you may be absolutely certain that you know exactly what is in every pile and where all your possessions are, but if you start intermixing piles, pretty soon you're going to forget where things are (assuming you knew where they were in the first place).

When you eventually decide to start throwing things away, you may come to an intermixed pile and find a check for a hundred dollars from your insurance company. This reinforces your belief that you need to comb through piles before throwing items away.

Even if you found a check for a hundred dollars, would that check be worth the shame, embarrassment, isolation, and all the other negative consequences of your hoarding?

Fear of Memory Loss

Within hoarding, there appears to be a connection between fear, clutter, and memory (Frost and Hartl 1996). Most hoarders tend to think *Out of sight, out of mind* and thus use clutter to help themselves remember their possessions better. This helps explain why hoarders often have empty shelves and closets.

Again, we come back to fear. Most hoarders do not have memory deficits, but are afraid to trust their own memory. We have heard many hoarders say, "If I do not see my possessions, I will forget about them." Because of the quantity of items hoarders possess, they may forget where something was placed or whether it existed in the first place. Have you ever forgotten what shows you taped, how many bottles of ketchup you have, or where the Halloween ornaments are that you bought two years ago?

You may assume that because you forgot about a possession, you have a bad memory. If you think you have a bad memory, you are more likely to check your possessions. By checking your possessions more frequently, you are deceiving yourself into thinking you have a memory deficit. You may count the ketchup bottles, or spend time looking for the ornaments, or just acquire more items because you don't know where to start looking.

Lack of Organization

Do you find it impossible to organize your belongings? Do you feel overwhelmed, not knowing where to start? Do you wonder whether you were always a disorganized person or things just got out of hand? Let us review what may have happened to you.

Let's imagine that you like to own jewelry. You have an assortment of different types of jewelry: gold, plastic, silver, and combinations, and the jewelry varies in value from inexpensive to expensive.

Initially, you were able to sort your jewelry and put it away, but as time went on, it got more and more difficult. You thought of more categories, like type of piece (bracelet, necklace) and personal value to you. As these different classification variables were introduced, there were so many different ways to categorize your jewelry that you became overwhelmed and just started making piles without trying to categorize the pieces.

This is a fairly common process among hoarders. It becomes a very dangerous cycle of clutter, especially as more and more items are brought into the mix. The bigger the piles become, the more overwhelmed you feel in trying to organize them. Many hoarders seem to have problems with categorization, and they develop piles and piles of similar items even though they feel like they have different objects.

Exercise: Identify the Traits

You can do this exercise in your notebook or here in the book. Following is a list of traits and a series of hoarding situations. Your goal is to name the correct trait for each situation. Each trait will be used only once. The answers are listed at the end, but try not to look at the answers until you are finished.

Traits

instrumental saving

aesthetic value

sentimental saving

fear of losing information

indecisiveness

fear of making mistakes

inability to prioritize

fear of loss

worries about memory

lack of organization

Situations

1. Joe sometimes picks up soda tops from the street because he likes the way they reflect sunlight.

2. Megan fears that people will ask her about current events, so she keeps hundreds of newspapers in her kitchen and will discard them only after she reads and understands the stories.

3. Pat has tried on several occasions to get rid of her piles, but every time she tries, she gets overwhelmed and doesn't know where to start. So she convinces herself that she'll figure it out next time and never makes progress.

4. Steve keeps his paycheck stubs from the past twenty years in case he is ever audited by the IRS.

5. Kelly really wants to watch her brand-new television but will only set it up when she finds the perfect wall unit to put it in. She fears getting the wrong wall unit, so her television is just sitting on the floor.

6. Mark has hundreds of old pizza boxes in his kitchen. He saves them because they remind him of the good times he had when friends came over and ate pizza and watched sports games with him. He really misses those times.

7. Michelle has five filing cabinets in her house, but they are all empty. She has literally thousands of papers to file away but can't figure out how to classify them.

8. Karen has piles and piles of clutter in her house, consisting mostly of papers and mail. Her sister wants to come over and clean up for her, but Karen is deathly afraid that her sister will mistakenly throw away something important.

9. Todd has clutter all over his house, but his closets and storage spaces are completely empty. He is afraid that if he puts his possessions away, he will forget about them.

10. Mary has approximately one hundred pairs of shoes, but she can never decide which pair to wear, so she just wears the same pair every day.

Answer Key

1. aesthetic value

2. fear of losing information

3. inability to prioritize

4. instrumental saving

5. fear of making mistakes

6. sentimental saving

7. lack of organization

8. fear of loss

9. worries about memory

10. indecisiveness

3

Reasons to Seek Treatment

Your life is filled with possibility. Reach high, look forward, and never give up. The world is waiting for you.

—Marian Wright Edelman

In chapter 1 we discussed compulsive hoarding from a few different angles, one being a basic sociological perspective. This chapter will delve into significantly greater detail about how hoarding affects people sociologically. We will outline several reasons why it is important for you and your family to seek treatment.

Perhaps you already know quite well why it's important to seek treatment. However, you may be unsure if your hoarding or the hoarding of a loved one is significant enough to warrant treatment. If you feel that you have a good understanding of the reasons to seek treatment, you may want to just skim through this chapter. However, if you think that your hoarding behaviors are not problematic, or that they are not significant enough to warrant treatment, then we suggest you read through this chapter carefully. You may gain some valuable insight and motivation to work on your hoarding. Although hoarding manifests differently in different people, it affects those around you greatly. Keep in mind that even if you don't feel distressed about your hoarding, your spouse, children, friends, and neighbors most likely do.

Quality-of-Life Issues

When looking at the effects of any psychological or psychiatric condition on a person, one must consider the level of disruption that the condition creates in the person's life. This is certainly true in the case of compulsive hoarding. In order to understand hoarding fully, you need to look at how the hoarding has affected your life overall. The following sections will outline the various ways that compulsive hoarding can affect your life.

Lack of Functional Living Space

One of the most common effects of compulsive hoarding is the reduction—and sometimes elimination—of functional living space. What exactly is functional living space? Look around your home. Is the furniture being used as storage for clutter, or can you comfortably sit on it? Are you able to use your stovetop and kitchen countertops, or are they covered in clutter? Can you walk freely in your home, or do you have to make pathways in the clutter in order to navigate around? Do you and your children have comfortable beds to sleep on?

Having functional living space means being able to use your furniture, floor space, closets, and countertops for their intended purposes. It is very common for hoarders to have limited and sometimes no functional living space in their homes.

This lack of functional living space certainly will affect your quality of life, primarily because you will not be able to enjoy your home. Rather, your home becomes a giant unorganized closet used solely to store your possessions. If you are not able to use your kitchen to cook meals, then you probably rely on ordering food from outside sources. You may be taking in more calories by eating out frequently, which may cause you to gain weight. Certainly, ordering out a lot can cause a financial strain also. If you have a family, you are not able to enjoy meals together, and your children can't invite friends over for supper.

Many hoarders become socially isolated because having others see their clutter embarrasses them. This embarrassment generally applies to strangers as well as friends and family. For example, it is relatively common for hoarders to not let repairmen into their homes to fix broken appliances.

Getting Additional Storage Space Does Not Help

Some people think that the problem is not the hoarding per se, but rather insufficient storage space within the home. So their solution is to acquire additional storage space such as storage lockers, storage chests, garages, trunks of automobiles, basements or attics, yard space or sheds on their property, or even additional homes or apartments.

These additional spaces may initially work out as storage solutions, but it's usually just a matter of time before these spaces become filled with disorganized new possessions and new clutter. In fact, we have worked with hoarders who owned their homes but rented several apartments for the sole purpose of storing their possessions. In each of these cases, the person eventually learned that the problem was not a lack of space but rather a lack of the skills to clean, organize, and maintain their possessions.

Unhealthy Living Conditions

It is possible that if you live amidst clutter and have little or no functional living space, your possessions and clutter may be causing and maintaining chronic medical conditions in those who live in your home. In our experience, people who live in clutter are more likely to experience the following medical conditions than those not living in clutter:

- headaches

- respiratory problems (asthma, coughing)

- allergies

- fatigue or lethargy

- insomnia or sleeping difficulties

Furthermore, people who live in cluttered homes often take many different types of allergy and headache medications with little to no relief. You may be asking yourself why these conditions exist more frequently and why medications are not as effective. The answer is that the sources of these ailments are not addressed by medications.

The sources of these ailments are the dust, dirt, molds, and fungi that exist underneath and throughout clutter. The only way to fully alleviate these medical conditions is to remove the source of the problem. However, if you are not able to vacuum your floors because of significant clutter occupying floor space, then the dust, dirt, molds, and fungi not only exist but may also multiply.

If you are not able to clean countertops, desks, dressers, or windows, these places may contribute to the problem as well. Oftentimes, hoarders are not able to clean up routine mishaps such as spilled drinks or knocked-over plants because clutter prevents them from successfully accessing the spills. Along the same lines, food can become rotten, either because it is inaccessible or because it is covered by clutter and thus invisible.

There are additional dangers in those homes that have pets. Sometimes dogs are not able to get to their owners in time to indicate the need to go outside to go to the bathroom, or they are not able to navigate the clutter successfully in time, and as a result the dog urinates or defecates in the home. Cats may not be able to access their litter box because of excessive clutter.

There is a serious health concern to be aware of in homes where cats are allowed to go outdoors and indoors freely. *Toxoplasmosis* is an infection caused by a parasite found in the feces of infected cats. You can become infected if you accidentally touch your hands to your mouth after gardening, cleaning a cat's litter box, or touching anything that has come in contact with cat feces. You can prevent infection by washing your hands with soap and water after cleaning the litter box, but if your cat is defecating outside the box, you could be at greater risk. Toxoplasmosis affects those with weakened immune systems and may cause birth defects or mental retardation if a pregnant woman becomes infected.

Unsafe Living Conditions

When you consider the lack of functional living space and the development and maintenance of chronic medical conditions caused by dust and other allergens, you can begin to understand how a hoarder's home can become a dangerous place to live. However, these components are only a part of what can make a hoarder's home dangerous.

In fact, there many more reasons an excessively cluttered home could be objectively viewed as a dangerous place. First, bearing more weight than it is built for may structurally damage the flooring of homes. This extra weight comes from excessive possessions, specifically newspapers, magazines, boxes, heavy machinery, and extra appliances. For example, you may not think too much about the weight of your stacks of newspapers and magazines. However, a stack of newspapers that reaches three feet in height may weigh upwards of fifty pounds. Then multiply the weight of each three-foot stack of newspapers by the number of stacks, and the total weight may be much greater than you assumed. The total weight of the newspapers alone may weaken floorboards if left untouched for months or years. If those newspaper stacks were exposed to a spilled drink or some type of water damage, the flooring would be under even more pressure and could decay more rapidly.

One of the more severe safety concerns in the homes of hoarders is that of fire hazards. Hoarders' homes are more likely to be filled with numerous flammable items. Take for example the stacks of newspapers and magazines we mentioned above. Even a cigarette ash could ignite a whole pile of newspapers. If that happened, the fire would be very difficult to manage because of the number of highly flammable items within close proximity. Possessions blocking doorways and windows could prevent people from safely leaving the home in case of a fire and could also prevent emergency personnel from entering.

Possessions may be blocking radiators or vents, causing poor air circulation. Heat-sensitive items placed too close to the radiator or furnace may catch fire. Also, when radiators happen to be blocked by clutter, they may become damaged. Hoarders may then buy and use space heaters during the winter months. The surfaces of space heaters can reach very high temperatures and can easily cause a fire if a flammable item is placed too close to the heater.

Also, pools of water, rotten food, or animal waste may become breeding grounds for vermin, mosquitoes, cockroaches, and other uninvited creatures. Any home that attracts rats and cockroaches could certainly be viewed as unsafe, especially if there are children living in the home.

Exercise: Is Your Home Functional, Safe, and Healthy?

Below is a list of questions that we would like you to go through to determine how much your daily living has been affected by your hoarding and to what degree your home may be a health hazard. Answer the following questions honestly. You may want to have your notebook handy in case you want to take notes or make reminders to yourself.

Remember that clutter in your home can prevent you or your family from engaging in various activities. Please answer yes or no as to whether these activities are affected by your hoarding. If you have even some difficulty, answer yes.

Can you do the following activities?

Y / N   cook in your oven

Y / N   cook on the stove

Y / N   eat at the kitchen table

Y / N   use the countertops

Y / N   put items into cupboards

Y / N   use the kitchen sink

Y / N   wash dishes in the dishwasher

Y / N   do laundry

Y / N   use stairs with ease

Y / N   sit on every chair or sofa in the house

Y / N   sleep in your bed

Y / N   find things easily

Y / N   use all toilets

Y / N   use all showers

Y / N   clean the house

Y / N   allow repairmen into your home

Y / N   do paperwork at a desk or table

Y / N   your children can play in the house freely

Y / N   entertain people at the house

Y / N   use the trunk or backseat of the car

Now think whether your home is safe. Answer yes or no to the following questions.

Y / N   Is the staircase filled with objects?

Y / N   Are the entrances to the house blocked?

Y / N   Are the boilers or heaters surrounded by objects?

Y / N   Is there mold in some rooms?

Y / N   Is the cleanliness of the house compromised?

Y / N   Have dirt and allergens built up?

Y / N   Is there insect infestation due to clutter?

Y / N   Is the paint peeling?

Y / N   Are there pathways instead of empty space to walk?

Y / N   Is there animal waste in the house?

Y / N   Is there spoiled or expired food in the house?

Y / N   Are there exposed electrical cords?

The Involvement of the Legal System

Now that you understand the extent of the problems hoarding can cause, it may make sense to you why the legal system sometimes becomes involved. In severe situations where there are fire hazards and where living conditions are dangerous for adults and children, law enforcement officials may intervene. We have worked with several families whose homes have been condemned and whose possessions have been forcefully removed by the county or state and thrown into Dumpsters. In fact, this is becoming more common.

In some states (New York, Washington D.C., and Wisconsin) as well as in Ottawa, Canada, there are task forces set up to deal with the legal issues surrounding hoarding behavior. More and more public health agencies are becoming aware of the complexities of hoarding and the need to deal with it in a special manner.

The task forces help prevent inappropriate interventions and coordinate efforts between county officials and those who hoard. You may be surprised to learn that attorneys, police officers, fire chiefs, child protective agencies, insurance personnel, animal welfare agencies, and guardians of the elderly are all involved in understanding and working with the problem of hoarding.

Years ago, before hoarding was recognized as a psychological problem deserving of compassion, the courts would order a hoarder to vacate the house or apartment. When the person was unable to do so, the courts would just send over a county Dumpster, clean up the home, and often throw the person out on the streets. You can imagine how devastating that would be for anyone, and especially for people who have difficulty parting with their possessions.

Insurance companies began to refuse to pay claims related to fires started in cluttered homes. Liens were put on these homes, and little or no profit was made when the homes were sold.

There were people who committed suicide after they were evicted and all of their possessions were thrown into Dumpsters. Other people and animals died in their own homes because they were unable to escape fires. Others, including the elderly, were living on the streets with nowhere to go after being evicted. Tragedies like these brought awareness of the problem of severe hoarding to the county and state level.

We recognize that these are severe cases of hoarding. However, milder forms of hoarding can also cause serious legal problems. Spouses of hoarders often seek divorce, and custody battles begin. Spouses take pictures of the home to show the judge that the home is unsafe for their children. Sometimes, child protective agencies are called to investigate whether the child is being properly taken care of. Children may be removed from the home if the agency determines that there is neglect (for example, no functional space, vermin, allergenic mold due to broken pipes, objects blocking exits or staircases, or improper nutrition). There is a risk assessment in all of these cases. The legal system will intervene if county fire and housing codes are not followed.

Do not be frightened by all the legal ramifications, because agencies are now aware that hoarders need treatment, not punishment. As long as you understand and are willing to engage in treatment to overcome the problem, the legal system will work with you.

The Effects of Hoarding on Family Members

As you can imagine, those who live with you may not see eye to eye with you regarding your possessions. For many spouses and children of hoarders, there are two sources of conflict. One is living amidst clutter and having little or no functional living space. Your loved ones feel it is not their home any longer. They have very little say over how their own belongings are ordered or arranged or what they would like their own home to look like. They too may feel embarrassed.

The other source of conflict is that they may want to live with you but believe that it is not feasible. Often spouses consider divorce or separation. Some only separate their quarters, while others actually file for divorce. Adult children move out, and younger children fantasize about the day they can move out. Besides these devastating effects, family members may also become involved in the legal ramifications of hoarding.

This section will discuss the problems that family members endure and will give some suggestions about how to get treatment for a loved one. Both you and your family members can benefit from reading on. You can perhaps begin to empathize with and understand your family, and they can learn more about the problem and what they can do to not feel completely overwhelmed and powerless.

Clutter Causes Familial Problems

Sometimes it is difficult for hoarders to understand why their family members are not more supportive about the hoarding. Sometimes hoarders believe so strongly in their thoughts and attitudes about the need to have possessions and the acceptability of living in clutter that they are not able to understand how others could feel or think differently.

However, family members do think and feel differently about clutter. Hoarders tend to justify clutter and the lack of functional living space by telling themselves that the positives of having the possessions outweigh the negatives of clutter and no functional living space. In fact, they adapt and learn how to live in clutter and without the "luxuries" that nonhoarders are privileged to have. They often make excuses about not having the time to organize, blame others for causing or adding to the clutter, or say they gave up trying to keep a "clean" house because no one appreciated it anyway. Resentments seem to run both ways.

Although the justification about the clutter may make sense to the hoarder, very often the justification does not work for family members, primarily because they do not have the same desire or need to have so many possessions and are therefore only able to see the negatives of the situation. The only positive factor they can weigh into the situation is their love for the hoarder and the hoarder's personal characteristics outside of the hoarding. Spouses and children of hoarders are able to see beyond the hoarding and identify a good person underneath all the clutter, but sometimes that is not enough. You may love someone but not be able to live with that person.

Families Have Difficulty Functioning in Clutter

In the beginning, while the clutter is still manageable, family members may not even notice the extent of the problem. They may think that because possessions are so important to their loved one, they will learn to adjust and accommodate. However, as clutter builds, so do negative emotions about living in clutter and losing functional living space. This can lead to disagreements and arguments about the hoarding, often without resolution.

As time goes by and the intensity of the hoarding increases, family members begin to feel more and more frustrated. They tend to become more isolated, and they are not able to enjoy their lives as they once did.

Children lose the ability to play freely in the home. Their play areas slowly become filled with possessions and clutter. Adolescents may lose their desire to invite friends over to the house because of embarrassment. The parent with the problem may not allow anyone in the house. This message is sometimes very direct and sometimes subtle. Either way, family members learn not to invite anyone over. Even if no one says anything, the resentment begins to build. After all, the family can no longer use the house the way they want or the way most people do. The family members begin to feel that the imposition is too great and the hoarder is too controlling. The non-hoarding spouse may fear for the safety of their young children and even for themselves. Elderly family members sometimes fall over items and sustain injuries. Families have to make pathways through clutter in order to get from room to room. The difficulties may seem endless and hopeless as the clutter builds in volume.

Hoarding Can Cause Financial Problems

Many hoarders experience debt and have arguments with their families about money. As the need or desire to acquire more items increases, the hoarder may purchase items without considering their cost. Ongoing excessive purchasing may cause significant financial problems. If the hoarder is financially dependent, he or she may object to not having easy access to money. Perhaps credit cards have been taken away or only a set amount of money is put into a joint account. Items that are actually needed may not be purchased because there is no room for them. Once the problems begins, it snowballs.

Furthermore, as we mentioned earlier in this chapter, sometimes hoarders will acquire additional storage facilities to accommodate the increasing number of incoming possessions and the decreasing amount of functional living space. These additional storage spaces can often be expensive, especially when hoarders rent additional apartments or move into larger, more expensive homes. Over time, even self-storage space becomes extremely costly. These financial constraints often lead families into significant debt, disputes with collection agencies, and even bankruptcy.

Clutter Causes Anger and Resentment

The love and respect that family members have for their loved one who hoards is often not enough to make them feel that it is acceptable to live in clutter without functional living space. When people are forced to live amidst clutter, they often end up feeling angry, frustrated, resentful, hopeless, depressed, and guilty. These emotions may lead them to do things out of spite, things they might not otherwise do.

For example, many times family members will get angry and start arguments over minute, trivial things just to express their anger and resentment. Other times they pick legitimate arguments about the need to clean up the home and discard the excessive possessions. In the times when the hoarder agrees, they may try working together in cleaning up the home, but this usually leads to more fighting. The nonhoarding member is usually not allowed to make any decisions about what to save and what to discard. The hoarding member is perceived once again as having total control. More hostility may build up.

This may lead the family members to feel more intensely than they did previously. If the resulting emotions are increased anger and frustration, they may try to throw possessions away when the hoarder is sleeping or not home.

However, when this happens and the hoarder finds out that possessions were discarded without consent, the hoarder is likely to feel violated and lose trust in the family members. In some cases, this may even cause increased paranoia and lead the hoarder to guard possessions, check garbage cans, and keep a higher level of vigilance in order to prevent nonconsensual discarding.

In other cases, when the resulting emotions are increased depression and sadness, family members may experience a cycle of helplessness. Family members feel that no matter what they say, try, or do, they will not have an impact on the situation, and they feel more despondent and helpless than before. This may lead them to feel more depression, social isolation, and general malaise.

For these reasons, many hoarders' spouses file for divorce or separation. They often feel that the level of emotional turmoil, combined with chaotic clutter and no functional living space, is just too much for a family to endure. Often these divorces and separations end in bitter custody battles and lead to ongoing anger and resentment. In many cases, the hoarder is not equipped to cope effectively with these emotions and looks to the hoarding as a source of comfort.

We know that stress can exacerbate and intensify the symptoms of OCD and other anxiety-based disorders. The same is certainly true of hoarding. When hoarders experience bitter divorce proceedings, they often acquire even more possessions and become less willing to discard them. The whole process becomes painful for everyone involved.

Families May Seek Treatment First

For all of the above reasons and more, it is fairly common for the family members of a hoarder to seek treatment for themselves before the hoarder does. This can be beneficial for a number of reasons.

Certainly, if the spouse or children are feeling depressed or angry, those issues need to be worked on for their own personal benefit. If the goal of the family is to find ways to bring a resistant hoarder into treatment, then their own mental health is a crucial factor.

Obviously, the stronger and healthier they are, the better they will be able to handle potentially difficult situations later on when confronting the hoarder. The more family members learn about hoarding and what the treatment entails, the more likely they will be able to help get the hoarder into treatment.

Getting a Resistant Hoarder into Treatment

It is not easy to get a resistant hoarder to engage in therapy, and it is often a family member who contacts a therapist first. Family members often feel worse than the hoarder, who believes the clutter is not too bad and intends to clean it "one of these days." For the family, "one of these days" is not good enough, because the day never comes.

We have found the *intervention* technique quite helpful. We have adapted a strategy used to address substance abuse. Family members and friends sit down with the hoarder and explain that the clutter has gotten out of hand, talk about how it is impacting everyone's life, and explain that help is available. Family members should first become acquainted with what type of therapy is appropriate and who in their area can provide it, and preferably have an appointment set up for the day of the intervention.

One by one, each member of the intervention group addresses the hoarder and explains what they observe, why they are concerned, and that they are not judging in any way but merely trying to help. Everything should be said with love and genuine concern but, at the same time, firmly. The goal is to bring the hoarder to someone who can help. After that, the professional will guide you.

Often family members have to meet with the professional several times prior to implementing the intervention technique. It is not easy for family members. They are often scared and frightened of what will ensue when they confront the family member with the hoarding problem. By the time a family member seeks help, the clutter is usually out of hand.

Sometimes family members learn of the problem accidentally. For example, someone who has lived alone needs to be hospitalized, and when a family member goes to the house to pick up belongings, they discover the state of the home. Or a hoarder is on vacation, and a neighbor or friend decides to go look after the house. While walking around the outside, they notice the clutter in the house or in the shed through the windows. Or family members notice that they are never invited to the house. They get suspicious and make a surprise visit.

When someone accidentally finds out and confronts the person, one of two things will happen. Either the person will admit that the hoarding is a problem and immediately agree to receive help, or, more commonly, the hoarder will become embarrassed and withdraw from the person who discovered the hoarding. Here again, the intervention technique will need to be used when discussions and pleas to get help do not work.

Getting a resistant hoarder into treatment is not an easy task and will take time. Family members need to be firm, helpful, and—most importantly—patient.

4

Treatment Options

There are many ways of going forward, but only one way of standing still.

—Franklin D. Roosevelt

Now you know what compulsive hoarding is, how it affects others, and why you may be acquiring and saving your possessions. You're probably getting eager to start working on your symptoms and clearing your clutter. But before we do that, we need to discuss your treatment options and the motivational issues that may hinder your progress in treatment.

One of the very first things we do when a patient comes into our office is ask *Where do feelings come from?* It may seem fairly simple on the surface, but it is actually a very difficult question for some people to answer. The answer will be a crucial ingredient in the recipe for your treatment.

What's your answer? Many people reply *the heart*. Well, where in the heart? Is there a valve or chamber that is responsible for feelings? We're sorry, but the answer is no.

If you answered *the heart*, don't feel badly; you are certainly not alone. Interestingly, there is a widespread idea in human society that feelings come from the heart. In fact, many expressions in the English language reflect this:

> He's all heart
> From the bottom of my heart
> She has a big heart
> A heart-to-heart talk
> It comes from the heart
> The heart of a champion
> A heart of gold

On Valentine's Day we send heart-shaped chocolates and candies to our valentines. But even though society seems to think that feelings come from the heart, in reality, they do not.

If you answered *thoughts*, you are correct or at least partially correct. Actually, our feelings come from both our thoughts and our actions.

Cognitive Behavioral Therapy

Cognitive behavioral therapy (CBT) is a practical, hands-on approach that helps people change the way they feel by evaluating and changing the way they think and act. It is the combination of two different types of therapy: *behavior therapy* and *cognitive therapy*.

Behavior Therapy

When we tell people that one of the treatment approaches we use for hoarding is behavior therapy, they sometimes respond with comments like *I don't want to be like a robot* or *Isn't that used for animals?* Unfortunately, behavior therapy sometimes gets a bad rap. Behavior therapy has its roots in the work of scientists performing experiments with animals. But as the scientists began to better understand the principles they were studying, they began applying the principles to people. There are two central concepts in behavior therapy: *classical conditioning* and *operant conditioning*.

People often associate behavior therapy with Ivan Pavlov's 1927 dog experiment. Pavlov observed that whenever he presented his dog with food, the dog would salivate. He discovered that an internal response was conditioned to occur by an external stimulus. This is classical conditioning.

Let's say that you have an eccentric friend, and whenever that friend greets you, he hits you on the arm. After the first time he hit you, your arm was bruised and hurt. Then the next time you saw him, as he began to extend his hand for a handshake, you automatically became frightened and flinched. You flinched because you associated your friend's arm with fear and moved involuntarily.

In 1938, B. F. Skinner discovered that animals and people respond to either reinforcement or punishment from our environment. This is operant conditioning. Reinforcement can come from a variety of sources, including money, hugs, kisses, praise, and food. Reinforcement is the single most effective way to increase a behavior. For example, if you are teaching your dog to sit, then every time you say "sit" and she does, you should give her a treat. The more consistently you reinforce her sitting, the more likely she will sit when you say so. Punishment, on the other hand, is the most effective way to stop a bad behavior, and it can include removing privileges, loss of money, and yelling.

If you have children, you are probably well aware of how reinforcement and punishment work. If your child studies for her tests and does well on her report card, you may reinforce her accomplishments by giving her lots of praise, extra phone time, or some money. If, however, your child does not study and gets poor grades, you may punish him in some way, perhaps by taking away the car keys or removing video game privileges. Either way, your response will influence your child's future behaviors.

Exposure with Response Prevention

Exposure with response prevention (E/RP) is a treatment technique that comes from the classical conditioning paradigm. *Exposure* means that you place yourself in anxiety-producing situations repeatedly. While in these situations, you refrain from doing the compulsions or rituals that you would normally do to ease the anxiety; this is *response prevention*. You're probably wondering why in the world you would do that. The answer is that if you give the anxiety a chance to disappear on its own, it will. This process is called *habituation*.

Imagine jumping into a cold swimming pool on a hot summer afternoon. What is your initial reaction? You're cold, but if you stay in the water for a few seconds, your body gets used to the temperature change and you no longer notice it. Your body habituates to the cold.

Let's say that you have obsessions (unwanted, intrusive thoughts that cause great anxiety or discomfort) that while you are at work, your spouse is going through your possessions and discarding them without your consent. The compulsion you engage in to reduce that anxiety is to call home to check on your spouse, or to go home and see for yourself, or to check the garbage can later.

If you allowed yourself to tolerate the anxiety from the obsession and *not* do the compulsion, the anxiety would eventually go away by itself. This can be a very difficult proposition, though. We will help you through this process in the next few chapters.

Cognitive Therapy

You may be saying to yourself, *Well, exposure and response prevention sounds great, but I don't have any obsessions.* Remember that hoarding is often associated with OCD, but it may also occur by itself. Not every person who has trouble with hoarding will have obsessions. This is where cognitive therapy comes into the picture. In fact, everyone can benefit from cognitive therapy, whether or not they have obsessions.

Cognitive therapy was initially developed in the 1960s by Aaron Beck as a short-term method for treating depression by teaching people to recognize their dysfunctional thinking and think more rationally. Other researchers have created variations of cognitive therapy. Today, cognitive therapy and its variants are used to treat conditions including OCD, panic disorder, post-traumatic stress disorder, the eating disorders, and personality disorders (Beck 1995).

How Behavior Therapy and Cognitive Therapy Interact

How we think affects the way we feel, which affects what we do. What we do then affects how we think, thus affecting our feelings, and so on. Oftentimes, our thoughts and actions become intertwined and spiral in either a positive or a negative direction. Confused? Here's an example of the interaction between thoughts, feelings, and actions.

Imagine that you come home from a hard day at work. As soon as you open the front door, you notice piles of papers and boxes scattered all over the kitchen table, countertops, and floor. You tell yourself something like *I'll never get the kitchen cleaned. I'm hopeless!* Immediately after saying that, you feel overwhelmed, frustrated, and depressed. You tell yourself that you'll go lie down on the sofa for ten minutes. But then twenty, thirty, fifty minutes go by. You tell yourself that you should go clean it up, but you can't and you feel

even worse about yourself. Because you feel even worse about yourself now, you decide to spend more time on the couch because it
doesn't matter anyway. Later on, when the phone rings, you notice
that you've spent over two hours on the couch and are even more
disgusted with yourself for not having gotten up and cleaned, or at
least tried to clean, which leads you to feel even more depressed and
overwhelmed. And so on.

Does this process sound familiar? It's a very common scenario
and a good example of how our thoughts, feelings, and actions are
all interconnected and influence how we feel. Noticing and changing
what you say to yourself—your *self-talk*—is one of the most critical
parts of CBT. Your inner dialogue is one of the things we will target
in order to help you become a more rational thinker and feel
differently.

Exercise: Identify Your Self-Talk

In your notebook, write down the words *Think, Feel,* and *Do* on the
same line. Draw a vertical line down to the bottom of the page after
each word, so you create a table.

Imagine that you are in one room of your home right now. Try
to visualize the clutter. What are your thoughts? How do you feel?
When you enter this room, what do you typically do? Write down
your reactions in each of the three columns. Try this same exercise
for every room in your home that has clutter.

The Goals of CBT

By using CBT, you will be able to work toward and achieve
your goals. We have identified seven goals for you in the treatment
of your hoarding. If you can think of other goals, write them down
in your notebook.

- increase functional living space in your home
- create appropriate storage spaces for possessions
- correct irrational thinking
- maintain treatment gains (prevent relapse)
- improve family relations
- improve decision making and organizational skills
- improve quality of life

Getting Motivated

Since you're reading this book, you obviously feel some degree of motivation to work on your hoarding. But you may also have some concerns about how successful the treatment will be, whether you will follow through with it, or whether you are capable of changing. Maybe you have already tried to clean up your clutter and felt overwhelmed, frustrated, or angry. Maybe you have tried to change your hoarding behavior without success and are skeptical about your ability to change now. Maybe you are motivated to work on it but feel you don't have enough time to make the changes.

These motivational concerns (and others) are very common among hoarders. The good news is that we have some strategies and techniques to help you challenge these concerns and increase your motivation.

Exercise: List the Pros and Cons

First off, you need to list the pros and the cons about making changes in your life. Take out your notebook. On a blank page, write the word *Pros*, then draw a vertical line down to the bottom of the page. On the other side of the vertical line, write the word *Cons*. Fill in both sides with as many things as you can think of. Below are just a few of the responses we have heard from people who have done this exercise.

Pros

I'll have more space to walk around.

I'll be able to see my floors again.

I'll be able to sit on the sofa, put my feet on the coffee table, and actually watch the television.

My family will be more supportive.

I can have friends over to the house again.

Cons

I'll miss my possessions greatly.

I'll feel anxious, upset, or frustrated.

I might miss going to sales and buying the things I need.

Motivational Strategy: Say Out Loud, "I Am Not a Highway Construction Worker!"

If you have ever driven in New York, you know that there are lots of highways, parkways, and roadways, and they are frequently under construction. The problem with this highway construction is that it seems as though there is no well-thought-out plan as to how to execute the projects. On any given day, you might see ten different construction sites on a fifty-mile stretch of road. The state starts one project, then realizes that they need to get something else completed five miles down the road before the current project can go on, so they start another project. They seem to jump from project to project and never make any real progress on a given site. This is very frustrating for drivers.

This is similar to the churning phenomenon we mentioned in chapter 2. Churning is one of the most common sources of frustration and decreased motivation for change in hoarders. If you are going to successfully clean up your clutter, you will need to work on one target area at a time.

By telling yourself that you are not a highway construction worker, you will be reminding yourself to stay focused on what you are doing and leave that "site" only when the project is completed. This is a motivational strategy in the sense that it makes your task more manageable, and it's also a treatment strategy that we'll discuss further in chapter 6.

Motivational Strategy: Set Realistic Goals

One of the most common traps that hoarders fall into is setting unrealistic or impractical goals. For example, if you have ever tried to tackle an entire room (or even your entire home) in one day and expected to end up with a clutter-free area, you probably felt overwhelmed, frustrated, or angry.

You need to set realistic and attainable goals if you are going to be successful with anything in your life, especially cleaning up clutter. For instance, this book took us about one year to write. Although we knew the material very well, it still took us a long time to put it into a format that would make sense to readers. We sat down every week and set realistic goals for that week. A typical goal was to write five pages in a week. How do you think we would have felt if the weekly goal was to write five chapters instead? Probably overwhelmed, frustrated, and angry!

Motivational Strategy: Use Grandma's Rule

Another one of the traps you may have fallen into when attempting to work on the hoarding is deceiving yourself into thinking you'll clean it up "later." The *Premack principle* of behavior therapy states that you will be most successful in completing any task if you work on it first and then reward yourself with a pleasurable activity later. This is sometimes called *Grandma's rule* after the old lesson of eating your vegetables before eating your dessert.

Think about it. If you ate your dessert first, how likely would you be to eat your vegetables later? Not very likely at all. How about with children? What are the chances a child would study for a test *after* playing video games? Not likely. A much more effective strategy is to offer the video games as a reward for studying. This way, the child is significantly motivated to study because the reward will follow.

Have you ever told yourself that you'd start to clean up the clutter after you watched a movie, or after you made a call, or after anything else pleasurable? If so, then you probably never really got around to the cleanup and felt overwhelmed, frustrated, and angry.

Exercise: Set Aside Some Time and Identify Your Rewards

This exercise is a good way to combine the two previous motivational strategies. Look at your calendar and block out some time for the treatment program. (We'll talk more later about what you'll do during this time.) You don't need a whole week, month, or year. You can make progress in just thirty minutes a day. Write down in your notebook the days and times you have set aside for the treatment. On the next page, list some things you can do as rewards for following through *after* each treatment time. Keep in mind that your reinforcements don't have to be major; they can be very simple. Sometimes people have difficulty thinking of possible reinforcements, so below is a list of some common rewards:

- watch thirty minutes of television

- eat your favorite food

- call a friend

- read a book, newspaper, or magazine

- go for a walk

When to Consider Seeking Professional Help

We believe the treatment program we outline in this book can be very successful in helping you with your compulsive hoarding. The CBT program is the core of the treatment. We understand that you may have been living with your hoarding for a long time, and this treatment may be somewhat difficult for you to adhere to. For this reason, we have included techniques and suggestions to help you stick to the program and give you the best possible chance of success.

However, there may be variables beyond motivational issues that impair your ability to follow through with the treatment. If you are experiencing any of the following conditions or feelings, you may want to consider taking medication under the care of a psychiatrist:

- severely depressed mood

- dependence on or abuse of alcohol or drugs

- extreme anxiety (such as frequent panic attacks or agoraphobia)

- thoughts about suicide or hurting yourself

- moderate to severe OCD symptoms not related to hoarding (handwashing, checking locks or doors)

- hallucinations or delusions

What Medications Are Available?

This section on the medications used to treat hoarding is to be used only as a reference guide. If you think you could benefit from medication, we strongly recommend that you seek the care of a psychiatrist.

Believe it or not, one of the first medications ever used to treat a mental disorder was marijuana, which was used in France beginning in 1850. Ever since, many types of drugs have been used to treat psychiatric disorders.

Currently, there are no hoarding-specific medications. The medical approach to treating hoarding is based on the premise that OCD and hoarding are interconnected disorders. Therefore, many of the medications used to treat hoarding are the same medications used to treat OCD and related disorders.

These drugs are divided into different categories: antidepressants, antipsychotics, anticonvulsants, antianxiety agents (including hypnotics or sleeping agents), and stimulants. Overall, these medications affect the brain by either reducing its hyperexcitability or stimulating its hypoexcitability.

There are six major questions to be considered whenever you think about trying a medication:

Why are you taking the medication, or what is the clinical indication?

What is the best dose for you?

What are the possible side effects?

What complications could result from using the medication during pregnancy?

What other medications are you taking, and how might they interact with the new medication?

What are the possible toxic or lethal effects if you take the medication in excess (overdose)?

Another issue to consider is the cost of medications and the possible limitation that cost can have for you. In today's competitive market, drug prices are constantly changing, and some medications can be quite expensive. Be sure that you inquire about the costs of medications, and ask your insurance provider what they cover before you agree to start medications. Many medications are available in a less expensive generic form. Ask your psychiatrist if there is a generic form that would be appropriate for you.

In our discussion, we will use the commercial or trade name of each drug because that is what you are most likely to be familiar with. Just bear in mind that if you go to the pharmacy with a trade name prescription, your insurance company may want you to purchase the generic brand.

Antidepressants

You do not have to be depressed to be taking antidepressants. Antidepressants are often prescribed for anxiety, insomnia, pain, and a whole host of other problems. The history of antidepressants as we know them today goes back to the 1950s. You probably know someone who is taking an antidepressant. After all, there are more people suffering from depression than any other problem.

Antidepressants are the medications of choice when treating OCD and related disorders. They act by increasing the response to an external input that causes a happy or euphoric change. These drugs manipulate the availability of two major neurotransmitters, serotonin (which we discussed in chapter 1) and *norepinephrine,* which seem associated to the mechanisms that control depression and anxiety.

Antidepressants are typically prescribed for major depression, OCD, anxiety disorders (including panic disorder, agoraphobia, and generalized anxiety disorder), eating disorders (anorexia nervosa and bulimia), pseudodementia, enuresis (bed-wetting), and night terrors.

There are three major categories of antidepressants: *selective serotonin reuptake inhibitors* (SSRIs), *tricyclics,* and *monoamine oxidase inhibitors* (MAOIs).

SSRIs

SSRIs work by affecting the brain's regulation of serotonin. Currently, they are quite popular because they are believed to cause fewer bothersome side effects than the tricyclics and MAOIs. Perhaps you know someone who is taking one of the common SSRI medications: Prozac, Luvox, Zoloft, Effexor, Paxil, Celexa, or Lexapro. Some of these medications can be taken once a day, even once a week, in pill or liquid form.

Tricyclics

In spite of the recent popularity of SSRIs, tricyclic antidepressants are once again becoming popular because they are quite effective. Some common tricyclic medications are Elavil, Tofranil, Surmontil, Pamelor, Vivactil, Doxepin, and Anafranil. The one you would most likely be prescribed for hoarding is Anafranil. Anafranil has been around for a very long time, and it was the first medication approved to treat OCD. Although it is within the tricyclic category, Anafranil is considered a partial serotonin reuptake inhibitor. In other words, it works somewhat like a SSRI.

MAOIs

These antidepressants act by blocking the action of the enzyme *amine oxidase.* There are three well-known MAOIs: Marplan, Nardil, and Parnate. A MAOI is prescribed when a patient is not doing well on a tricyclic or an SSRI. Tricyclics and SSRIs should not be taken with MAOIs because they could cause your blood pressure to skyrocket. In fact, if you are on an MAOI, you have to follow a special diet avoiding a substance known as *tyramine* (found in aged cheeses, air-dried sausages, fava beans, sauerkraut, chocolate, Chinese food, and some alcoholic beverages) so that your blood pressure does not go up.

Major Side Effects

When they are considering starting a new medication, many people worry about side effects. However, while the prescription insert lists a whole host of side effects, do not forget that not everyone is going to experience a side effect. Most side effects disappear within a few days when your body gets used to the medication. The most common side effects of antidepressants are fainting, low blood pressure, dry mouth, constipation, weight gain, sexual problems including anorgasmia (difficulty having an orgasm), liver damage, difficulty urinating, and possibly glaucoma. They sound scary, but keep in mind that if you do have side effects, something can usually be done about it. Your doctor will combine your medications with others, reduce the dosage, give you an entirely different medication, or give a medication to control the side effect.

Are Natural Substances of Any Value?

There are some natural substances that have antidepressant properties, including vitamin B_6 and amino acids like L-tryptophan and DL-phenylalanine. Another natural antidepressant can be found in the herb Saint-John's-wort. Herbs like Saint-John's-wort are typically used to treat mild depression, and the literature has been inconclusive about its effectiveness. No research has been done investigating the effects of Saint-John's-wort on compulsive hoarding.

Before running off to your vitamin shop, you should seek the advice of a psychiatrist. Just because a product is labeled "natural" or "herbal," it is still a chemical and can have side effects, toxic effects, and even fatal effects, so please be careful.

Antipsychotics

The antipsychotics are medications that work in the brain by modifying the levels and availability of neurotransmitters, mainly dopamine and serotonin. The first antipsychotics were available in the early 1950s, and they have evolved over the years.

These medications are primarily used to treat patients with psychosis. However, your doctor may also give you an antipsychotic medication, in small dosages, to help you to see your hoarding problem from a different perspective. You do not have to be psychotic to receive an antipsychotic medication.

For example, if you firmly believe that you would be nothing without your possessions and that your possessions completely and totally define you, you see no problem with your clutter, and you blame others for your inability to organize your stuff, then an antipsychotic may be helpful. Not only would the antipsychotic medication give you a different perspective, it would actually help you tackle the problem better.

If you do not think your hoarding is a problem but the clutter is, in fact, severely interfering with your life (for instance, you may lose your spouse or your family is in danger), then the antipsychotics may help you gain insight into the problem. In other words, if you have absolutely no doubts and are 100 percent confident that your life would be miserable without your possessions, an antipsychotic medication may help you to question that belief a little more easily. Most likely you would only have to take a small dosage, probably in addition to an antidepressant.

Some commonly used antipsychotic medications are Risperdal, Orap, Haldol, Zyprexa, and Geodon. With very small dosages, you are not likely to experience major side effects. Some possible side effects include muscle contractions, parkinsonism (tremor, shuffling gait), low blood pressure, dry mouth, constipation, blurred vision, nasal congestion, and sedation.

Anticonvulsants

Anticonvulsants may be prescribed in order to stabilize your mood. If you are the type of person whose mood goes up and down and you experience difficulty controlling your moods, you may be prescribed an anticonvulsant for your mood along with an antidepressant for your hoarding behavior. Some well-known anticonvulsants are Tegretol, Klonopin, Depakote, Neurontin, and Dilantin. Some possible side effects are low blood pressure, dizziness, nausea, diarrhea, constipation, and dry mouth.

Antianxiety Agents

You have probably seen movies in which people offer each other Valium or Xanax to relax, cope with stress, and get over a relationship or some hardship. In fact, antianxiety pills are prescribed to deal with anxiety. You may be prescribed an antianxiety medication if you have difficulty sleeping, are under a lot of stress, have family problems due to your hoarding or for some other reason, are worried about things in general, or just had something bad happen to you.

Antianxiety agents do not specifically target your feeling that you need to hold on to your possessions, but they can be very helpful if you are excessively anxious about discarding items. Common antianxiety medications include Xanax, Ativan, Valium, Klonopin, Buspar, Tranxene, Serax, and Catapres. Possible side effects include low blood pressure, dizziness, fast heartbeat, irregular heartbeat, dry mouth, diarrhea, and menstrual irregularities. If you are having trouble sleeping, you may be prescribed Ambien, Sonata, Dalmane, Restoril, or Halcion. You should not be taking sleeping pills for long, because they can be addictive. Most sleep problems are caused by depression and anxiety anyway.

Stimulants

In children, stimulants slow down the excitability of the cerebral tissue; conversely, in adults, stimulants increase cerebral excitability. You may be asking yourself why you would be prescribed a stimulant for hoarding. In some cases, hoarding appears to be related to *attention deficit disorder* (ADD). The treatment for ADD is usually some type of stimulant. This does not mean that if you are a hoarder you definitely have ADD, nor does it mean that ADD is the reason for your hoarding behavior.

If your hoarding is related to ADD, a stimulant may be helpful. Common stimulants are Ritalin, Concerta, and Adderall. Some possible side effects are weight loss, irritability, insomnia, palpitations, nausea, dizziness, and constipation.

The treatment of hoarding with medication is relatively new, and the results are moderately favorable. For most people, the combination of cognitive behavioral strategies with one or more of the medications we have discussed in this chapter may be the most effective approach.

5

Applying Cognitive
Strategies

Change your thoughts and you change your world.
—Norman Vincent Peale

Now that you understand what the treatment options are for your hoarding symptoms, you are ready to start the active treatment phase. This chapter is going to help you look at and better understand your thoughts about your hoarding. It is very likely that you have been thinking about your possessions and your hoarding for a long time. You may have even defended your thoughts about your inability to discard your possessions from the challenges of others. Changing your thoughts and beliefs about your hoarding, and thus changing your feelings and behaviors, can often be a difficult and strenuous process.

Your understanding of the concepts and strategies in this chapter is crucial to your success in overcoming hoarding. Therefore, you may need to read this chapter a few times and practice the techniques repeatedly until you feel confident with them. If you proceed too quickly from this chapter to the next one, the treatment may not be as effective.

Our goal in this chapter is to help you identify what types of distortions you make in your thinking and in what situations you make them, and to teach you how to become a more rational thinker. This will help you to change not only your attitude toward your hoarding but also all the unpleasant feelings associated with the thought of giving it up. If you practice the strategies we teach in this chapter, you will begin to see that controlling your hoarding is not as awful and catastrophic as you once thought.

Understanding Your Thoughts from a Cognitive Therapy Perspective

One of the core features of cognitive therapy is becoming aware of your thoughts, because your thoughts are often so automatic that you don't even know they are present. Your self-dialogue is habitual or routine, and you are probably not aware of the actual thought processes involved. If you think a certain way most of your life, those thought processes become a part of you. You don't give it much thought, and you believe there is no other way to think.

In other words, when something happens to you, you may think it is the event that is causing you to feel upset, angry, hurt, or happy, but this is because you are not aware of your actual thought processes in that situation. We will show you that it is your beliefs, attitudes, values, and evaluation of the event—not the event itself—that lead you to experience an emotion and behave in a particular way.

You may be saying to yourself that you don't really have thoughts in a given situation, you just react. However, if the environment had the power to make you feel an emotion, then everyone would feel the same emotions. We certainly know that different people react differently in the same situations.

Whether or not you are aware of your thoughts, you are always thinking. If a thought is not within your awareness, then it is most likely an *automatic thought,* one that you have had so many times before that you no longer pay much attention to it. For that reason, it appears as if you are reacting rather than thinking.

When you have unhealthy, maladaptive, irrational, or faulty thoughts, you are likely to experience negative emotions. You are left feeling depressed, ashamed, angry, overwhelmed, or defeated, all without really understanding why.

Think about it. If you are having a negative conversation with yourself in your mind, then you are likely to feel badly afterward. How many times have you been in an argument with someone else and felt great during the argument and afterward? Your internal dialogue will greatly influence how you feel, whether you are aware of that dialogue or not.

Cognitive therapy is designed to help you identify situations that may bring up those unpleasant automatic thoughts, identify the types of distortion the automatic thought incorporates, and challenge those thoughts. By doing this, you will improve your mood, self-esteem, confidence, and motivation.

Identify Your Thought Patterns

The first step is to identify situations that are likely to lead to automatic thoughts. Cognitive therapy is based on the idea that your emotions, thoughts, and beliefs are intertwined and related. Your thoughts are predictable and consistent responses to the situations you are in. You have a pattern of thinking that is based on your attitudes and beliefs about many things. Once you identify the patterns of thinking that upset you, you can change the thoughts. You will need to learn new ways of looking at the same situation, and this in turn will help you feel better.

Thoughts may be triggered either by being in the situation or by simply imagining the situation. People often create images in their mind that are as powerful as being in the situation. For example, close your eyes and imagine looking at a serene lake. What feelings did the image bring up? What were you thinking while imagining the lake? If you felt calm or happy, maybe you thought of happy childhood memories or how beautiful life can be. However, if you felt sad or frightened, you might have thought of being alone or rejected, or drowning with no one to rescue you. You can see that images or actual situations will lead to different emotions based on your assumptions about the situation.

Let's imagine that you just came home from a doctor's appointment. What thoughts immediately enter your mind when you open the front door to your home? It's very possible that you have thoughts like *Look at this mess! I'm such a loser* or *I'll never be able to clean this clutter up* or *This hoarding is killing me* or *If only my family would be more helpful and put their stuff away, we would not have clutter.* These are fairly typical automatic thoughts that enter people's minds when they look at clutter.

What emotions would you feel if these thoughts entered your mind? You might feel depressed, sad, frustrated, overwhelmed, embarrassed, or angry. Perhaps you've had this experience: You're away from home, and you think about where you might have placed a possession or whether your possessions will be exactly where you left them when you return. You begin to have thoughts like *I hope my spouse didn't move my stuff around while I was out. It just isn't fair! Others should respect my belongings and not touch them.* Then you feel angry. Further, the more you accept those thoughts as being true, the more intense and disruptive the resulting emotions become.

Here are examples of situations that might trigger your automatic thoughts and emotional responses:

- looking at clutter

- going to a garage sale

- reading a magazine or newspaper

- shopping at the supermarket

- shopping for clothes

- being handed a free flyer

When you are in these and other situations that cause automatic thoughts, the thoughts are likely to be inaccurate or irrational in some way. Very rarely do people have automatic thoughts that are completely and unequivocally accurate.

Consider the automatic thought that you're a loser because you have clutter. Is this thought absolutely 100 percent true? Are you really a loser because you have clutter? If so, then you are suggesting that there is no means of measuring your self-worth other than whether or not you have clutter. How then would nonhoarders measure their self-worth? Certainly not all nonhoarders are "winners" simply because they don't hoard.

Logic tells us that there are many ways besides hoarding status to measure self-worth, including your compassion for others, trustworthiness, sense of humor, and so on. As you can see, the thought of being a loser is simply a thought. Your thoughts are not automatically true simply because they enter your mind.

Think about it in a situation independent of hoarding. If you are a fearful flier and the plane you're on is experiencing turbulence, what thoughts would automatically enter your mind? You might think that you will die or that the plane will crash. Does that mean the plane will actually crash because you thought about it? No. If you ask an expert for a list of reasons that airplanes crash, we guarantee that you will not see automatic thoughts listed.

Unfortunately, the fact that automatic thoughts are not automatically true also holds for positive thoughts. Even if you think to yourself that there is a million dollars in your wallet and you repeat that thought ten times, you won't find the money in your wallet. Thoughts are always only thoughts.

Exercise: Identify Daily Situations That Create Automatic Thoughts

Trying doing this exercise over a period of a few days rather than in one sitting. This way you'll have a greater understanding of your own thoughts and emotions.

In your notebook, divide the page into three vertical columns and label them *Situation, Emotion,* and *Automatic Thought.* Under *Situation,* write down a situation that often brings on emotional states and automatic thoughts. Then, in the column labeled *Emotion,* list the emotions you feel in that situation and rate the intensity of each emotion on a scale of 1 to 100, with 100 being the highest possible intensity. Finally, list the automatic thoughts in the next column, being as specific as you can. Repeat this process for every situation you can think of that causes automatic thoughts.

For example, under *Situation,* you might write "Came home from appointment and saw clutter immediately when I opened the front door." Under *Emotion,* you might list "overwhelmed (85), depressed (90), frustrated (75)." Under *Automatic Thought,* you might write "Look at this mess! I'm such a loser," "I'll never be able to clean this up," and "This hoarding is killing me."

Cognitive Distortions

Now that you have an idea of the types of situations in your life that create automatic thoughts, you are ready to take the next step in your cognitive therapy. As we've said, automatic thoughts are likely to be inaccurate or irrational in some way. In cognitive therapy, we refer to inaccurate or irrational automatic thoughts as *cognitive distortions.* In this section, we'll describe each type of cognitive distortion and explain how it can relate to hoarding.

All-or-Nothing Thinking

All-or-nothing thinking is also referred to as *black-and-white thinking* because it describes the tendency to think in extremes. Although everyone thinks in these terms sometimes, all-or-nothing thinking is prevalent in people with OCPD and in hoarding.

This type of thinking paves the way for perfectionism. When you fall short of perfection, you may tell yourself that you are worthless or that your life is meaningless. The people who seek perfection tend to be the unhappiest people, because they constantly fail to achieve their goals. This usually results in depression or a sense of being incomplete.

Examples:

My whole life means nothing without this possession.

I am stupid (or a loser, or worthless, or pathetic) if I throw something away.

If I can't find the perfect spot for this item, I'll be miserable.

Overgeneralization

Overgeneralization occurs when you interpret one negative experience as a lifelong pattern of misery. You think that bad things always happen to you and that positive things rarely, if ever, happen. You focus only on the negative aspects of experiences and then tell yourself that they always happen to you.

Examples:

My coupons for the supermarket expired, so I had to pay full price for the groceries. I have terrible luck.

I once threw out a valuable item. Therefore, if I am not extremely cautious, I will always discard things of value.

Mental Filtering

In *mental filtering*, you pick out one negative detail of an experience and dwell on it so much that it darkens your outlook on the whole experience.

Examples:

I put away all of today's incoming mail except for that one insurance invoice I couldn't decide what to do with. I'm such a failure! I can't even figure out a simple bill.

I got most of the clutter on my bed cleaned up, but there's still that pile of clothes that need to be put away. I'll never be able to get this finished.

Discounting the Positive

Discounting the positive occurs when you reject positive experiences by insisting that they don't count, they were expected of you, or you achieved them because of luck and not because of ability. By doing this, you maintain a negative outlook despite positive experiences.

Examples:

I know, today I sorted the mail and put away the important stuff instead of procrastinating and letting it pile up. But I should do that every day. The only reason I could do that was because there were only a few letters today.

I only cleared off my bed enough to be able to sleep on it, but other people don't have anything on theirs.

Jumping to Conclusions

When you *jump to conclusions*, you interpret experiences negatively without any solid evidence. There are two forms of jumping to conclusions.

Fortune Telling

Fortune telling occurs when you think that you can accurately predict the future.

Examples:

I know exactly what will happen if I try to clean the clutter. I'll feel overwhelmed and frustrated. So why bother? I'll save myself that misery by procrastinating.

I will never be able to keep the dining room table cleared off, so why bother?

My family is upset with me, and no matter what I do, they will never see me in a different light.

Mind Reading

Mind reading is sometimes referred to as *thinking for someone else*. Generally, you misinterpret another person's body language, tone of voice, facial expression, or demeanor and then base your thoughts on that interpretation.

Example:

Because the clerk counted the cans I purchased, she thought I was a freak.

My husband came home from work and looked disappointed. It was probably because of the clutter.

Magnification and Minimization

When you engage in *magnification* or *minimization,* you either magnify or minimize the problem.

Examples:

My house will never be clutter-free, and my family will always hate me for it. (Magnification)

My house is just a little messy, and I am not the best housekeeper. (Minimization)

Emotional Reasoning

Emotional reasoning occurs when you confuse a feeling with reality. You don't distinguish between your emotional state and your personality traits or characteristics. For example, when you feel depressed, you tell yourself that you're a depressed person. This is especially common in people with depression, OCD, anxiety, and hoarding.

Examples:

I feel overwhelmed and out of control, therefore my problems are not fixable.

I am an anxious person, and I will never be able to be calm.

Should Statements

Should statements are distorted expectations that you set for yourself. They use absolute terms (*should, have to, never, always, must, ought to, can't,* or *impossible*) and are based on unrealistic standards. When you incorporate these words into your expectations, you will inevitably feel angry, frustrated, depressed, or guilty.

Examples:

I should be able to clean up the clutter with no problems.

I never do anything right.

I should be able to find everything I need immediately.

My wife should be more understanding and leave my stuff alone.

Labeling

Labeling is a distortion that results from overgeneralizing and thinking in black-and-white terms. When you label, you call yourself a pretty nasty name because of a mistake or bad experience, but you mean that name as a trait or characteristic. If you tend to start sentences with *I'm a (bad name here)*, you're probably engaging in labeling.

Examples:

I'm a loser because I have clutter in my home.

I have not been able to give my family what they need, and therefore I am a failure.

I have difficulty making decisions, so I am inadequate.

Others are better than me.

Personalization and Blame

Personalization and blame generally occurs when you confuse influence over a situation with control of a situation. You may hold yourself personally responsible for a situation that you had little or no control over, and at the same time fail to recognize the real factors that were responsible for the situation.

Example:

My husband spilled coffee on himself while sitting on the sofa. There is clutter around the sofa, so I guess it was my fault. I'm not a good person to live with.

Each of the cognitive distortions we've discussed in this chapter will cause you to feel some sort of negative emotion, and thus cause you to avoid or put off cleaning up your clutter, just feel badly about your hoarding, or merely justify your hoarding behavior. The more excess negative emotions you have, the less likely you are to change. For that reason, it is important to change your thoughts and feel better about yourself and your capabilities so you can change your behavior.

Very often, people engage in different cognitive distortions in different situations. For example, you may tend to think in black-and-white terms when you're alone but jump to conclusions when you're around other people. Throughout your treatment, it will be important that you have a good understanding of the types of cognitive distortions you engage in and the situations that cause them.

Exercise: Identify Your Cognitive Distortions

Take out your notebook and find the Identify Your Self-Talk exercise from chapter 4, where we asked you to visualize the cluttered rooms in your house and write down the thoughts you had. Rewrite those sentences on a new sheet of paper now. If you can think of other thoughts, beliefs, or expectations that you have, write them down too.

Next to each sentence, write down the type of cognitive distortion you believe it to be. This will be helpful in future exercises. Please refer to the definitions of the cognitive distortions as much as you need to during this exercise. Some thoughts may incorporate more than one type of distortion.

Cognitive Therapy: Your Own Personal Scientific Experiment

One of the most common automatic thoughts hoarders have is *My possessions identify me.* By believing this thought, you are telling yourself that your possessions identify you as a human being. Although you may believe this to be true, the effect of believing it contributes to your depression and frustration. What would happen if you tested the validity of this thought in a scientific manner? Let's try it.

Think about yourself as a person. Who are you? What traits or characteristics define you? While it may be true that your possessions are important to you, they certainly are not the only things important to you, right? Your family, intelligence, values, ethics, morals, sense of humor, empathy, respect for others, and trustworthiness are also important parts of you.

But by saying outright that your possessions identify you, aren't you discounting all these other aspects of your life? You are disregarding those great traits and telling yourself that the only thing important to you is your possessions.

This pie chart represents a person who believes that his possessions constitute 80 percent of his identity. Is this how you view your identity? Do you think objectively that your personality really looks like this?

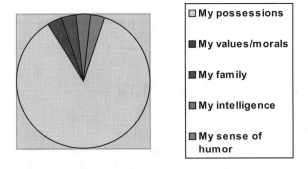

Before you proceed to the next section of this chapter, take a few minutes to complete the following exercise. It will be helpful for you to understand how much of your identity is constituted by your possessions before you learn how to challenge other cognitive distortions.

Exercise: Put Possessions in Their Place

Take out your notebook and start with a new page. For this exercise, you will probably need to erase as you go, so use a pencil and eraser. Label the top of the page *The Pieces of My Identity*.

Listed below are some things that generally tend to be important in people's lives. Feel free to add to this list. Your job in this exercise is to quantify how important each of these things is to you, or how much of your personality each of these makes up.

Assign a percentage value to each thing reflecting how important it is to you. Remember that you have only one hundred percentage points to distribute. You can't go over one hundred.

my possessions

my family (spouse, kids, parents)

empathy

respectfulness

my values, morals, and ethics

intelligence

my friends

my sense of humor

trustworthiness

my job or work

Changing Your Thoughts

The previous exercise is a good way to dispute your automatic thoughts about your hoarding behaviors. As you can see, your hoarding does not represent as much of your identity as you may have once believed. If you do in fact find that your hoarding defines the majority of your identity, you will need to reexamine that and start putting value on your other attributes.

What was once *My possessions identify me* can now become something along the lines of *My possessions are only a part of who I am. I value other things besides possessions.* This more rational statement probably would not have entered your mind had you not challenged the automatic thought.

One of the goals of cognitive therapy is to show you that if you interpret your automatic thoughts literally, you will feel more negative and intense emotions than if you challenge and question them. If you come from the perspective that your automatic thoughts are hypotheses, then you can determine how true or untrue they are, instead of automatically assuming they are true simply because you thought them.

Automatic Thoughts Are Hypotheses, Not Facts

In the last exercise, you treated the thought that your possessions identify you as a hypothesis, as you would in a science experiment. Remember how litmus paper works? If you dip a strip of litmus paper into a solution, the paper turns red or pink if the solution is acidic. The only way to know if the substance is acidic is to test it. In the same way, you can test your automatic thoughts. The only way to know if they are true or untrue is to test them.

Take a look at the list of automatic thoughts and types of cognitive distortions you made in the Identify Your Cognitive Distortions exercise earlier in this chapter. What kinds of cognitive distortions did you make? Look also at the automatic thoughts you listed. Do they appear to be nonnegotiable? You may believe right now that they are facts. Maybe you believe this because you have thought them so many times that there doesn't seem to be an alternative. Maybe you believe them because you haven't done the experiment; you haven't learned how to challenge them and think differently.

Conducting the Experiment: Challenging Your Thoughts

In this section, we will show you how to perform the experiment to test the accuracy of your automatic thoughts. All scientific experiments must follow the same steps in order to be considered valid and reliable. The steps are

1. State the hypothesis.

2. Perform the experiment.

3. State the findings.

The first step in your experiment is to state the hypothesis, or in this case, the automatic thought. Let's use one of the automatic thoughts mentioned earlier. So the hypothesis is *I'm a loser because my house is such a mess.*

The second step is to test the validity and accuracy of your automatic thought by performing the experiment. Ask yourself the following six questions and examine the answers to determine how valid the thought is. Really try to think of yourself as an objective researcher who is testing the validity of the hypothesis.

1. Is there any evidence that this thought is true? Is there any evidence that you are a loser? What is your definition of a loser? Do you consistently fail at *everything* you try? If so, you have never had a single success, only failures. That seems too harsh, right?

   Do you have good qualities or characteristics? If you are skilled at your job, or have ever succeeded at a task, then the idea of you being a loser is invalid. If you are not successful in one area of your life, it does not mean you are a failure in all areas and thus a loser.

   Do you have multiple sources of information suggesting you are a loser, or is that idea coming solely from you?

Are people literally coming up to you at work, on the street, or at home and saying, "You are such a loser"? If the idea that you are a loser is coming only from within yourself, then the validity of the statement decreases.

2. Ask yourself how this thought affects you. What emotions does it create when it enters your mind? You probably feel depressed, frustrated, or overwhelmed. Why wouldn't you? The thought says straight out that you're a loser, right? It makes sense that the outcome would be some sort of negative emotion.

3. Is there any other explanation for this situation? Are you saying that the only reason you hoard is because of this inherent loser personality? If so, you are implying that if you stopped being a loser tomorrow, your house and car would be impeccably neat and there would be no clutter. In other words, if we divided the world up into winners and losers, the winners would have beautiful, meticulously clean, orderly homes and the losers would all have clutter. That certainly isn't true. There are reasons for your hoarding behavior, but being a loser is not one.

4. If a friend or a family member had the exact same thought (stated the same hypothesis), how would you respond? Would you agree and say, "Yes, you are a loser because of your hoarding," or would you disagree with the statement?

    Interestingly, you are more likely to give supportive and rational advice to a fellow hoarder than to yourself. You would probably say that the person has many nice qualities and features and that her hoarding only represents a piece of who she is. In fact, everyone has strengths and weaknesses, right? Would you honestly tell your child or friend who thinks she's a loser that you agree?

5. Is this thought situation specific, or do you have it all the time? Surely it makes sense that if the automatic thought were true and you were a loser, you would think it constantly. So, does this thought come in while you're at work, while you're driving, or while you're in the shower? If the thought only enters your mind when you actually see or imagine clutter, then it is situation specific and less valid than if it were always present.

6. Ask yourself what your best friend (or parent or child) would say to you if you said the automatic thought aloud. This is similar to the fourth question, but it comes from a

different angle. If you went directly to your best friend in the world, whomever that may be, what response would you get? Would your friend agree with the thought or give you different feedback? If you have in fact gone to a friend with this thought, what response did you get?

The next step in your experiment is to state the findings. The information we gathered during the experiment is that there is no evidence (aside from the actual thought) that indicates that you are a loser. In fact, there is a good amount of evidence to the contrary. You are good at your job, you have friends and family members who care about you, and you have many positive qualities and characteristics. Further, the thought only enters your mind when you see or imagine clutter.

Developing Rational Responses: Practice What You Preach

The goal in developing a rational response to an automatic thought is to create an internal environment where you can see things more clearly. When your mind is flooded with automatic negative thoughts, it is quite difficult to see things clearly; your view will be clouded or biased. The effect of that bias is that you become your own worst critic. Developing a rational response allows you to take the role of a friend or coach, which is exactly what you need. If you would give supportive feedback to someone else with the same thought as yours, then you need to practice what you preach.

Take all the information you gathered during the experiment and pull it together now. Try to come up with a one- to three-sentence response to the automatic thought. For example, what would a rational and accurate response be to the thought *I'm a loser because my house is such a mess?*

Perhaps something like *Although I have clutter, there are other reasons for my hoarding behavior. I am working on taking control of my hoarding. I have many positive characteristics, and I have people in my life who love and respect me.* This type of response creates a more supportive and understanding internal mentality, which will cause you to feel less intense negative emotions.

You may not necessarily agree wholeheartedly with the rational response in the beginning, but the more you counter automatic thoughts with rational responses, the more you will believe them, and—ultimately—the more you will believe in yourself. The very opposite has already happened to you. Every time you had an automatic negative thought up until now, you didn't challenge it, and you believed it to be true. As a result, you have probably felt depressed, overwhelmed, angry, and frustrated. The more you think the irrational thoughts and believe them, the worse you feel.

Now is the time to reverse that process. Get into the habit of repeating the rational responses over and over again. The more you say them, the more you'll believe them and the quicker you'll feel better. In the next chapter, you will learn the behavioral techniques that will enable you to clean up your clutter. Imagine how much more successful you'll be if you have more self-esteem and challenge your automatic thoughts.

Again, the rational response is *Although I have clutter, there are other reasons for my hoarding behavior. I am working on getting control of my hoarding. I have many positive characteristics, and I have people in my life who love and respect me.* Think about the difference in outlook compared to the automatic negative thought *I'm a loser because my house is such a mess.* Doesn't it seem obvious which of these thoughts is more likely to increase your motivation to change?

Exercise: Develop Rational Responses

Take out your notebook and turn to the pages where you wrote down your automatic thoughts and indicated the type of cognitive distortions you made. For each of the automatic thoughts, go through the scientific process and test the validity of the hypothesis. Do the actual steps of the experiment on a separate page in the notebook. When you finish each experiment, state your conclusions and develop a rational response to that automatic thought.

Make a flash card for each automatic thought you test. Although you can do this in your notebook, we strongly recommend that you use index cards to make actual flash cards, because then you can easily view them while applying the techniques in the next chapter.

On the front of each flash card, write *Automatic Thought,* and below that *Cognitive Distortion.* Label the back *Rational Response.* Then fill in the automatic thought and the type of cognitive distortion it represents on the front side, and write the rational response on the back. These flash cards will be very useful throughout the cleanup and relapse prevention stages of your treatment.

For example, the flash card for the automatic thought we tested together earlier would look like this:

	Automatic Thought
FRONT	I'm a loser because my house is such a mess.
	Cognitive Distortion
	All-or-nothing thinking
	Labeling

	Rational Response
BACK	Although I have clutter, there are other reasons for my hoarding behavior. I am working on getting control of my hoarding. I have many positive characteristics, and I have people in my life who love and respect me.

Putting Together All the Steps

Let's go through another round of the experiment, but this time we will incorporate all the steps we outlined for you in this chapter. Try to follow these steps for every automatic thought you challenge:

1. Identify the automatic thought (hypothesis to be tested).

2. Identify the cognitive distortions involved in that thought.

3. Make the front of the flash card.

4. Perform the scientific experiment to test the validity of the thought.

5. Develop a rational response.

6. Fill in the back of the flash card.

Here is an automatic thought that is likely to enter your mind during the cleanup phase of the treatment: *I can't throw _____ away. I need it.* You can fill in the blank with any possession you feel you can't throw away. Let's say for this exercise that the possession in question is a bundle of plastic bags.

Step One: Identify the Automatic Thought (Hypothesis to Be Tested)

I can't throw away these plastic bags.

Step Two: Identify the Cognitive Distortions Involved in That Thought

- Should statements
- Jumping to conclusions

Step Three: Make the Front of the Flash Card

> **Automatic Thought**
> I can't throw away these plastic bags.
> **Cognitive Distortion**
> Should statements
> Jumping to conclusions

Step Four: Perform the Scientific Experiment

1. Is there any evidence that supports the idea that you can't throw the bags away? To say that you cannot do something implies that you do not have the ability to do it. Are you suggesting that you do not have the ability to throw the bags away? You have the ability to move your arms to the bags, make a clasping motion with your fingers, lift the bags, and throw them into the garbage. You can do it. You may not want to, but that is different than not having the ability. It might be difficult for you to throw the bags away, but you can do it. In fact, you have succeeded at other difficult tasks in your lifetime, perhaps at work or in raising children.

2. What emotions does the thought that you can't throw bags away create for you? You might feel depressed, frustrated, and possibly inadequate in some way.

3. What is the reason you hoard plastic bags? Is it because you are a loser, or because you have an erroneous belief that you will not be able to find a plastic bag in the future when you need one, or do the bags have some sentimental value?

4. How would you respond to a friend or family member who came to you with this very same thought? You probably would say something supportive, like "You have the ability to throw it away, but I know it's difficult for you."

5. Does the thought of not having the ability to throw plastic bags away occur in more than one setting or only when you are faced with the possibility of throwing them away? Most likely, you think about this only when you are cleaning clutter or when you have a bag in your hand and you have to decide what to do with it. If you walked around all day long thinking to yourself that you do not have the ability to throw plastic bags away, then the hypothesis would be more valid. In fact, you would not be able to throw any plastic bags away in any situation, not just at home.

6. What would your best friend say to you in response to this thought? Would he be critical of you and agree that you have no ability to throw things away, or would he be more supportive and understanding?

State the Findings

Pulling together all of the findings from the experiment, you have no evidence that you are unable to throw the bags away. If anything, you have evidence to the contrary. You do in fact have the ability to throw them away. You feel depressed and frustrated when that thought comes into your mind. You have many bags and could get one if you needed it in the future. You would give more-supportive feedback to someone seeking your advice on the very same issue, and the only time you think this thought is when you are in a difficult situation (cleaning your clutter).

Step Five: Develop a Rational Response

The advice that you would give to your best friend is usually a good place to start when you are trying to think of a rational response. Taking into consideration all the information gathered so far, a more rational response might be something like *Although it is likely to be difficult to throw these bags away, I can do it.*

Step Six: *Fill In the Back of the Flash Card*

Rational Response

Although it is likely to be difficult to throw these bags away, I can do it.

6

Cleaning Up the Clutter

The only way around is through.
—Robert Frost

By now, you're probably eager to get started on the actual cleanup of your clutter. In this chapter we'll walk you through a step-by-step approach to cleaning up and regaining functional living space.

Preparing for Success: A Few Tasks before You Clean Up

Before you begin cleaning, there are few steps you can take to make the process more effective. If you're going to put your blood, sweat, and tears into the cleanup process, you might as well make it as effective as possible, right? Actually, the more you follow our suggestions, the less likely any blood or tears will be necessary.

Try to Temporarily Suspend the Acquisition of New Items

Limiting the number of new items entering your home will help you be successful in cleaning up your clutter. Those of you who live in snowy climates know how frustrating it is when many inches of snow fall and it's your job to shovel. As the snow falls, you have to anticipate the best possible time to shovel your walkway or driveway. It can be very frustrating when you have just finished shoveling and it begins to snow again or a snowplow comes right past you and dumps all the snow from the street onto your freshly shoveled pathway. Your hard work is greeted with even more work to take on.

The same thing could happen to you during the cleanup phase of treatment. If you successfully discard items but then acquire an equal or greater number of new items, your work will be canceled out. If you decrease the number of new items entering your home, you will make more progress.

One thing you can do to immediately reduce the number of possessions coming into your home is to cancel subscriptions to magazines and newspapers. If you anticipate this being difficult, try using the cognitive therapy techniques from chapter 5 to break down your worries. If you think it will be impossible or close to it, don't worry about it for now.

If you don't want to completely eliminate all your subscriptions, try canceling half of your subscriptions, or at least one of them. Overall, the fewer new items entering the picture, the easier the cleanup will be.

If you feel confident that you can successfully limit the number of incoming items, then do so. If your main difficulty is with discarding items, and you don't have too many new items coming in, then you may want to just skim through the following section. If you are concerned that limiting new possessions will be very difficult, the next section will help you.

Create and Review Your Flash Cards

If you feel it will be difficult to reduce the number of new items entering your home, take out the cognitive therapy flash cards you made in chapter 5. Try to identify your exact thoughts about not acquiring more items. What types of cognitive distortions are you making?

Let's take a look at some common automatic negative thoughts regarding limiting acquisition. In previous chapters, we've discussed the just-in-case reasoning that is so common in hoarding. You may be thinking this way while you are shopping. For example, while shopping for groceries, you may purchase more items than you really need because you think there may be a need for them in the future. However, if your goal is to clean up your kitchen cabinets, and you are acquiring more items than you need in the moment, you will have a major conflict. This is like a snowplow problem: if you bought more items, you would be canceling out your progress in cleaning out the kitchen cabinets.

Let's say the automatic thought is something like *I should purchase more batteries just in case I need them in the future.* Referring to chapter 5 if you need to, go through the steps of breaking down this automatic thought. The cognitive distortions are should statements and jumping to conclusions. Then ask yourself the six questions that test the validity of the statement, try to create a more rational response, and make a new flash card. A sample rational response would be *I am working hard to control my hoarding, and it is important to me to limit my acquisition of new items. If I really need batteries in the future, I can buy them then.*

A common belief you may have is that you are stupid or ignorant if you do not read newspapers or magazines. This belief can incorporate all-or-nothing thinking, labeling, and should statements. Ask yourself the questions about the validity of the idea and create a more rational response.

Carry your new flash cards with you at all times, especially in situations when you are likely to have automatic thoughts. Read the rational responses out loud and repeat them five times (you can do this ahead of time or when you are actually in the difficult situation). This way, you are likely to have a less intense emotional response to the thought and you will be more likely to pass on acquiring the extra items. Create new flash cards for any automatic thoughts you have about other new items.

Practical Preparations

Now you're one step closer to beginning the cleanup process. Just a few more things, and you're on your way.

Get Some Boxes and Markers

First, you will need to find some medium-size storage boxes that you can use during the cleanup phase. These boxes should be in relatively good condition and have space on them to write a label. The number of boxes you will need depends on the extent of clutter in your home. For the first round of cleanup, you will need a minimum of three medium-size boxes and one smaller box.

Also, you will need some pens or markers to label the boxes. You will need to know what is in these boxes later on.

Perhaps you have already tried buying storage boxes, and they became part of your clutter. You may be saying, "Well, I have tried that before, and I know it doesn't work." Do not become discouraged. We are going to tell you how to attack your hoarding systematically so that your attempts will work. We are going to give you a step-by-step program to follow. We won't just tell you to buy storage boxes and begin organizing. This is a different way to approach the clutter.

Clear Some Temporary Storage Space

Next, you will have to make room for temporary storage of the boxes needed during the cleanup. Finding temporary storage space may be challenging if your clutter is extensive. If you have a room you can designate as temporary storage, do so. If not, try to clear enough space in a portion of a room.

In either case, you must make yourself two promises. First, you must promise that you will use the space only to store the boxes used during the treatment and that you won't put other clutter in this area. This is extremely important. The last thing you want is to mix clutter with newly organized possessions! Second, you must promise to remove items from the temporary storage space only when the treatment program tells you to. If you remove items prematurely, you will become overwhelmed and confused.

These two promises are so important, we want you to sign them.

I promise to use the temporary storage space only for the boxes used during the cleanup. I will not combine clutter with these boxes or store any other possessions in this space.

_____

(sign your name here)

I promise to remove things from the boxes in the temporary storage space only when the treatment program tells me to.
I will not randomly take things out of these boxes.

_____

(sign your name here)

Schedule Times for Cleaning

In your notebook, make a calendar of the next two weeks, including today. Think about the things that you will have to do in those two weeks, then schedule in times for cleaning. In the beginning of the cleanup process, you may want to schedule shorter blocks of time because the system will be relatively new to you. The more comfortable you become with the system, the more you will benefit from longer cleaning sessions.

For the first two weeks, try to schedule at least one thirty- to forty-five-minute block per day. If it is not possible to schedule time every day, try to schedule cleanup on as many days as possible. Try not to skip cleaning more than two days in a row. The more consistent you are in the cleaning, the more effective you'll be. Your skills will strengthen if you clean every day or every other day.

If you can schedule more than one block per day, that is fine as long as you identify them as several individual blocks rather than one long, continuous block. Space each block of work time with a break of at least fifteen minutes. For example, if you can schedule three blocks for a Saturday afternoon, schedule the first block from 12:00 to 12:45 P.M., the second from 1:00 to 1:45 P.M., and the third from 2:00 to 2:45 P.M. This way you give yourself enough time to work but also enough time to rest between blocks. If you schedule yourself from 12:00 to 2:45 P.M., you are more likely to become overwhelmed and frustrated, and clean less effectively.

Think about the importance of taking breaks in other contexts. Would you rather have a surgeon operate on you immediately after she operated on someone else, or would you prefer that she take a break before your surgery? How about flying in a plane? You would probably want a freshly rested pilot to fly the plane rather than one who had just flown for ten hours straight, right?

It is also important to know yourself. Are you the type of person who does better working a little at a time so that you don't give up or procrastinate, or are you the type of person who is better off putting in many hours and finishing the task before you get discouraged and overwhelmed? Pick the approach that matches your style, but make sure you stop to rest and reward yourself even if you put in long hours.

Don't Forget to Reward Yourself

Remember, you will be more likely to stick with a difficult task if you plan to reward yourself with a pleasurable activity immediately afterward. Be sure to do something enjoyable after each cleaning session.

Also, you want to keep yourself nourished and hydrated during the breaks. Be sure to eat foods that will give you energy, such as proteins, fruits, and vegetables. Also, try to drink lots of water. This will improve your effectiveness during the cleanup.

Cleaning Up Your Clutter, One Step at a Time

Read this entire chapter *before* you attempt to clean any portion of your clutter. It is extremely important that you understand the steps before you begin the program. Some of the steps may seem logical to you, and other steps may seem nonsensical. Ironically, it will actually be good for you if some (or even all) of the steps seem foreign to you.

How do you feel? Are you nervous, excited, scared, overwhelmed? Everyone is different, of course, but there is a good chance you're feeling a little bit of everything. If you stay consistent and follow the systematic and structured steps we provide, this treatment program can be very successful for you.

The remainder of this chapter outlines the steps that we have found to be the most effective in cleaning up clutter and maintaining your gains. Our program is based on the work of leading researchers Frost and Steketee (1998). We have made some modifications to Frost and Steketee's program based on our own research and experience. We are confident that, like our own patients, you will leave your hoarding behavior behind if you follow the program consistently and methodically.

The very first round of cleaning up will be unique because you are starting from scratch. Every round thereafter will be different because there will be various areas that require maintenance steps before you clean new areas. We will outline these steps for you now and give you a detailed discussion of each step.

In order for this program to work, you must understand and accept that your previous methods of cleaning clutter have been ineffective. It's time to try something new. It is okay to disagree with some of the steps involved; in fact, many people disagree with us when we begin this treatment program with them. But try to follow the steps exactly as we outline them here, even when you disagree with them. Your skepticism will fade as you begin to see progress.

In the field of social psychology, there is a phenomenon known as the *mere exposure effect*: the more you see, hear, or smell a new stimulus, the more you will like it (Zajonc 1968). Think about when you hear a song on the radio for the first time. You may not like it the first time, but the more you listen to it, the more it grows on you.

The same thing is likely to happen with our treatment program. If you are uncomfortable with it at first, hang in there. Pretty soon you'll begin to like it, especially as you see progress.

Step One: Select a Target Area

As we've said, the actual steps involved will change slightly after the first round of cleaning. The first step right now is to select a target area. After the first round of cleaning, this will become the second step. Selecting a target area can be a little trickier than it seems. There are some very important issues for you to consider when you select a target area.

Aim for Positive Visual Reinforcement: Seeing Is Believing

In the Identify Your Self-Talk exercise in chapter 4, we asked you to visualize the clutter in your home and then identify your thoughts and feelings associated with your clutter. What did you write? Most people feel a host of negative emotions when looking at their clutter. Nobody enjoys living in clutter. In fact, just seeing clutter can have an instant negative effect on your motivation, emotion, and outlook.

For this reason, it will be important for you to select a highly visible area to work on first. The end product from your cleaning will provide a stark contrast against the remainder of the clutter. This contrast will serve as a positive visual reinforcement and help to motivate you for the next project. When you have cleaned a highly visible area, you will immediately be able to look at it and say, "I did that" or "That looks great." This is the opposite of the effect clutter has on you.

You may feel that you want to start by targeting closed-in spaces such as closets, desk drawers, or cabinets, with the rationale that if you had more storage space, you could organize the remaining clutter into those spaces. However, if you start with less visible areas, you are limiting the amount of positive visual reinforcement you get in return. In the beginning, it is especially important for you to be able to see the positive effects of your hard work.

Regain Functional Living Space

We strongly recommend that you start the cleanup in areas that, when cleaned, will provide functional living space. This is another good reason not to start with drawers and closets. Chairs, sofas, beds, kitchen tabletops, desktops, and stovetops are nice places to start because you will be able to actually use those areas immediately following the cleanup. In fact, the more you use these spaces for their intended purpose, not for storage, the more likely you will be successful in keeping them clear. This will be very helpful for you throughout the treatment program.

When picking a target area, ask yourself what kinds of activities you really miss doing. Some people would really like to have meals with their family at the kitchen or dining room table, but haven't been able to because the table has been used for storage. Others would really like to sit in their favorite recliner, but haven't been able to because it is filled with clutter. Pick a space that you can use and enjoy.

The more rewarded you feel by the effects of the cleanup, the more likely you will be to continue with the treatment program. As your confidence grows, you will become more effective in your cleanup sessions. This is the opposite of what happened when you tried to clean up and just transferred clutter from one area to another and felt overwhelmed and frustrated. The more that happened, the less motivated you were to attempt the cleaning again.

Set Realistic Goals within the Target Area

Often hoarders will want to start with massive projects like an entire floor of a house or an entire room. Most of the time, tackling such a large project creates a bigger mess than what you started with. Generally speaking, the larger the project, the higher the likelihood of failing. You are much more likely to finish a series of small projects than you are to complete one large project. Remember, we did not write this whole book in one sitting. Between the three authors, it took us almost an entire year to finish it.

A helpful technique is to break down each larger project into several smaller ones. Break down rooms into fractions or sections. Look at your living room as ten to twenty small projects rather than one huge project. If one-quarter of a sofa is cleaned, it will have a more motivating visual effect than a completely cluttered sofa. Further, if you clean one-quarter of a sofa and are able to enjoy that functional living space, you will be more motivated to work on the next quarter.

Select a Project You Can Stick To

A common mistake that people make is to move from one unfinished project to another. Remember that when you break down projects into a series of smaller, more manageable goals, it is very important that you complete each project one at a time. In other words, do not leave half the sofa cluttered and half of it cleaned up. If you find yourself saying things like *Well, the kids can now sit on the sofa and watch television, and it is not important if the grown-ups have to sit on the floor* or *At least we can get to the microwave now, and that is all we really need in the kitchen*, think again. Although you may have an urge to start another project before completing the current one, you must stay focused until the entire target area is finished. Partial success usually does not work. It is helpful, and it certainly makes you feel better, but you need to keep pushing forward. Imagine how great it will feel to complete the whole project.

The more you stray from the target area, the more likely you will end up overwhelmed and frustrated. For example, let's say you target half of the kitchen table, and during the cleanup, you find a paper that belongs in the den. If you then put it in the den, you have left your target area and started a new project—just like the highway construction workers who start many projects but finish none. You need to finish your target area before you leave it and before you take on another project altogether.

That also goes for not jumping into other smaller parts from the current part. For example, if you are working on one-third of the kitchen table, you must complete that third before going on to a different third of the table. You must complete a whole project before moving on to another.

Exercise: Select Your First Target Area

Take out your notebook and write down an area of your home that you would like to target first in your cleanup. Be sure to break it down into several manageable projects, even if it is not a large project to begin with. Be as specific as you can. If you'd like to clear the sofa first, and your sofa has three cushions, list each cushion as its own project. If you'd like to tackle the kitchen table, list each quarter of the table as its own project. Remember to choose an area that will give you positive visual reinforcement and that you can stick to until completion.

Step Two: Assess the Items in Your Target Area

Now that you have identified your first target area for cleanup, it will be important to get a bird's-eye view of the items in that area. This will give you an idea of what to expect during the actual cleanup. Often, the more information you have about a task before starting it, the more effective you'll be at it.

This is true for any number of situations outside of hoarding. Teachers will often give their classes a brief outline of the material to be presented before going into the details of the information. This helps the students acquaint themselves with the information and gives them a better sense of what is expected. If you see a doctor for an examination or procedure, the doctor will outline for you the steps of the procedure so you are less nervous while it's actually happening.

The more information you have about a future cleaning session, the fewer surprises you'll face in that time. Now, this does not mean that you have to pick apart the target area and know exactly what its contents are. The goal of assessing items in the target area is to try to prepare yourself mentally. If you can tackle any automatic negative thoughts regarding your hoarding before the actual cleanup, then you're that much better off.

Without actually touching any of the items, simply jot down the types of items you see in the area. For example, you might write *random papers, pens and pencils, plastic bags, cardboard boxes, bills, newspapers, magazines.*

Prepare Your Cognitive Therapy Flash Cards

Once you know what is in the target area, consider your thoughts about the possibility of discarding many of those items. If you know that there are lots of magazines stored in the area and you start to worry that you don't have the ability to discard them, look at your cognitive therapy flash cards. If you have already made a card specifically for this fear, remind yourself of the types of cognitive distortions the thought entails and review the rational response.

If you did not already make a flash card for that fear, create a new one. Go through all the steps we outlined in chapter 5 and develop a more rational response to the fear. This way, you will have some logical, rational thinking at your side during a possibly difficult cleanup. Being prepared with a rational response is much better than trying to clean up and listen to automatic negative thoughts at the same time.

Take a "Before" Picture

Taking a picture (preferably an instant one) before you begin the cleanup will be helpful to you throughout the treatment program. Once the cleanup of the target area is completed, we will ask you to take an "after" picture. The contrast between the "before" and "after" photos will give you even more positive reinforcement and add to your confidence and motivation. You'll be able to say, "Look at the difference! I did that myself."

Exercise: Assess the Items in Your Target Area

In your notebook, make a general list of the type of items that are in your target area. Do not touch anything in the target area while creating this list. Simply get a bird's-eye view and write down what you see. If you have any automatic negative thoughts during this process, check your cognitive therapy flash cards. If you do not have a corresponding flash card, make one now.

Step Three: Begin the Cleanup Using the Three-and-a-Half-Box Technique

The *three-and-a-half-box technique* is the core of our treatment program and, if used correctly, it will be a huge asset for you. However, it may also be one of the more difficult parts of the program for you to get comfortable with. If you give it a fair and impartial chance, you will become more comfortable with it, especially as you experience success. The more closely you follow the guidelines, the more effective you will be in your cleaning.

This technique will help you make decisions about your possessions. Remember, for many hoarders, items come into the home and for some reason they do not get put away. You may say, "I'll just put it here for now" or "I'll put it away later" and never make a decision about where the item belongs. The more you do that, the more clutter develops.

The goal of the three-and-a-half-box technique is to attain functional living space first, then later to organize the possessions into their appropriate places. Remember that in an earlier section of this chapter, we asked you to clear some space to be used for temporary storage. You will use that space to store some of the boxes used during the cleanup. When a significant number (or all) of the target areas are completed, you will go back to those temporarily stored boxes and put away the possessions you have decided to keep. Of course, we will help you organize your possessions in chapters 7 and 8.

The Treatment Process

Our treatment program is a structured and systematic approach to cleaning up clutter. It is important for you to understand the treatment program before you start using it.

In the beginning, the program will address one item at a time. As you begin to feel more comfortable with the program, throwing things away may become significantly easier for you. At that point, you may decide what to do with several items at once if you wish, but until then, we will ask you to focus on one item at a time.

Hence, you will pick up one item and decide which of the three and a half boxes to put it into. You will continue to make decisions about one item at a time until the entire target area is completed. Now, if you have extensive clutter, you may be thinking that it could take forever to clean up your home. This is a common reaction when we discuss the program.

You will learn valuable skills with this program, and you will eventually be able to apply those skills with greater efficiency. In the beginning, however, your skills will be a little shaky and it may take you longer. If you consistently use the techniques we recommend, your skills will become more developed and you will spend less time cleaning up during your twentieth session than you did during your first session. Also keep in mind that change will happen over time, not overnight.

A second point about the treatment process is that you need to clean each target area to completion before you remove anything from the treatment boxes. You may be tempted to put things away while on a break from the cleaning sessions, but you must wait to unpack the boxes until we tell you to.

Remember that your first goal for the treatment is to regain functional living space and provide positive visual reinforcement. You will organize your possessions later on. If you are spending time during the cleanup sessions transferring clutter from one area to another, you will become overwhelmed and frustrated quickly, and you will be much less effective at cleaning.

The Three and a Half Boxes

As you have probably deduced by now, there will be three and a half boxes for you to use during the cleanup phase. It is your job to put each item you pick up into one of the boxes.

Save box. This box is for items that you want to save but that are not appropriate for permanent placement inside the target area. For example, let's say the target area is one-quarter of the kitchen table, and the very first item you pick up is a stapler. Unless your family has an unusual policy of keeping staplers on the kitchen table, this is not the most appropriate place for the stapler. Because you want to keep the stapler, you place it in the Save box.

You might feel the urge to get up, leave the target area, and put the stapler where you think it belongs, like the den. Instead of doing that, however, resist the urge to get up and just put the stapler in the Save box. There will be plenty of time later in the treatment to put items in their appropriate places. Remember, if you leave the target area before it is completed, you are not following the treatment program. In order to be the most effective cleaner, you need to resist the urges to leave the target area. This may be very difficult for you in the beginning, but you can do it! If you leave your target area, you are more apt to become involved in another area, not finish up what you started, become overwhelmed, and finally give up.

Display box. This box is for the items that you want to save and that belong in the target area. For example, again using the kitchen table as the target area, let's say you come across the salt and pepper shakers. You feel these items belong on the kitchen table. But the goal of cleaning a target area is to remove all the contents first, so it makes sense to place the shakers in the Display box. After the target area is complete, you can remove the shakers from the box and put them on the table.

Discard/Recycle box. The items you decide to throw away or recycle are to be placed in this box. Some people like to split the box into sections: discard, recycle, sell, and donate. Other people like to use a garbage bag for items to be discarded. Use whichever system feels best; there is no right or wrong style. However, be sure to be consistent with whatever system you use.

To-Do-Immediately Box. This is the "half box" in this program. It is to be used only for extremely important items that cannot wait to be taken care of later. For example, let's say you find an important form to be filled out for your child's school, and the deadline is the next day; or you find cash or a check; or you find your current tax return forms, and the date is April 14. You may put these items into this box. It is strictly for items that need immediate attention.

The potential downside of this box is that you may want to put things in this box as a way of avoiding deciding what to do with them. Or you may overestimate the importance of every item and want to put them all in this box. The most effective strategy is to use this box only for crucially important items that need attention within the next few days.

The same rules apply to this box as to the others, however. If you place an item inside this box, it stays inside the box until the target area is completed. After completing the target area for the day, you can focus on the contents of the To-Do-Immediately box. This would be the time to put the cash you found in your wallet, fill out the form for your child's school, and file your tax returns. Any project, however crucial, that does not need to be dealt with *immediately* goes straight into the Save box, no questions asked.

There are inevitably going to be items that will not physically fit into these boxes. For example, let's say you are cleaning the kitchen table and you find a VCR. Obviously you are not going to force it into one of the boxes. Instead, put the item next to the appropriate box.

Only Handle It Once

The treatment program itself is a relatively easy process. However, there is another rule that you need to understand prior to starting the cleanup. Steketee and her colleagues have come up with a nifty acronym, OHIO, which stands for *only handle it once.*

Remember that your pattern of saying, "I'll just put it here for now" has not worked for you and, if anything, has contributed to your overall clutter. Once you pick up an item and put it in the correct box, you are not allowed to pick it up again. Think of the item as having industrial-strength glue on it, and as soon as it hits the box, it is stuck in there forever. This technique will help you build confidence in your decision-making skills.

These Are Your Skills, Not Someone Else's

Have you ever had a friend or relative come into your home and do the majority (or all) of the cleaning for you? How long after that massive cleaning project were you able to keep your home free of clutter? If you are reading this book, chances are you did not maintain the gains. Why is that? Probably because you did not learn new skills in cleaning and maintaining your home. The only thing you learned is if you are going to have a clean home, you need someone else to do it for you.

In fact, many hoarders have had their friends and family members offer to come over and clean up the clutter for them. In many cases, friends and family offer to clean because they can no longer cope with the clutter themselves, or because they feel that the hoarder is simply incapable of cleaning up.

When another person cleans up your clutter for you, the clutter usually starts to rebuild. As this process happens, you probably feel more confused and angry and so are less likely to maintain the gains, and the clutter accumulates faster.

Think about this in a different arena. Imagine that your son is complaining to you that he is not very good in math class. You see him struggling with his homework, and because you want him to feel better, you "help" him with his homework by actually doing it for him. How will he perform on his tests if you are doing his homework for him? You might do very well on the tests, but he is the one who has to take them, and he will perform poorly. Wouldn't it be better for your son if you hired a tutor to help him learn math in a different way? By applying new strategies to his homework, your son would be on the way to achieving better grades.

The same is true for you. Think of this treatment program as a tutor helping you to conceptualize cleaning clutter differently than you did previously. The new strategies and skills you apply to your cleaning will help you achieve greater success than you were able to achieve using the old skills. Remember, the only way to maintain cleanliness in your home is for you to clean your clutter yourself, learning new skills along the way and continuing to apply them.

For these reasons, we prefer that you do the treatment by yourself. An advantage of you being the only one who will make decisions about the clutter is that there will not be any arguing or disagreements during the treatment program. The more smoothly the program proceeds, the more effective it will become. If you and your friend are constantly disagreeing about which box to put items in, the program will not be as effective.

What to Do When the Target Area Is Complete

After you have successfully put each item from the target area into one of the three and a half boxes, you still have a few miscellaneous things left to do.

Let's say that you have just completed the first quarter of the kitchen table. You need to proceed with the following steps:

1. Empty the To-Do-Immediately box and take care of the contents. Anything not immediately addressed goes straight into the Save box, no questions asked!

2. Properly dispose of the contents of the Discard/Recycle box. As soon as you have finished the To-Do-Immediately box, dump the Discard items into the garbage can (preferably one the garbage company will pick up immediately). If your community has a recycling program, place the items to be recycled in the recycle bins. If you live in a community that does not pick up recyclables, then you will need to bring the recyclables to a drop-off site. You can find the locations of such sites by contacting your local government or waste disposal offices. Set aside any items to be donated or sold in your temporary storage area.

3. The contents of the Display box will remain inside that box until the entire project (the whole kitchen table) is complete. You can use the same Display box for the remaining projects in the target area (the other three-quarters of the kitchen table). Once the entire area is clear, you can display those items.

4. Label the Save box to indicate what target area these items came from. For example, with a dark marker, write *first quarter of kitchen table* on the outside of the box. Underneath that label, indicate the general types of items inside the box. Please do not list everything in the box. For example, write *pens, insurance papers, plastic bags, etc.*

5. Put all the boxes into the temporary storage space you created earlier. These boxes will remain in that storage space until you begin the next target area. Also, if you are unable to complete the target area or need to take a long break, put these boxes into the storage space until you return to complete the project.

   If you need to leave a target area partially completed until a later time, you must promise yourself that you will not put new items in the partially cleaned area. You will need to preserve your progress. We cannot overemphasize how important it is to keep the area free of clutter.

6. Take a picture of the freshly cleaned target area. You can compare this "after" shot to the "before" shot to see what a difference your work has made. If you have an instant camera, write "I did this on (today's date)" on the developed picture. If you're not using an instant camera, try to get the film developed soon so you'll have the positive reinforcement right away.

   Keep those pictures with you if possible. If you begin to feel overwhelmed or sad, take out the two pictures and look at your accomplishment. This will help you feel better and motivate you to continue the cleaning.

Step Four: Maintain the Gains You've Made

After you have taken care of the items in the To-Do-Immediately box and temporarily stored away the other boxes, you should go back to the target area and view your progress. Look at your accomplishment! Be proud of yourself; you did that! Oftentimes, people will look everywhere else and say, "Yeah, but look at all this other clutter." This is a cognitive distortion: discounting the positive.

Although it may be true that there is more clutter than cleanliness, your goal was to clear that target area, and you succeeded in reaching that goal. If you can do it once, you can do it again and again and again. Now you know that you have the ability to clean clutter and reach your goals. From now on, the statement *I can't clean clutter* is not valid.

One of the most important things to remember is that the cleaned target areas are never to be used again as storage space for your possessions. If you resort to old, unhealthy habits and store items in cleaned areas, your hard work will disappear, and you will feel lost, overwhelmed, and hopeless.

In the beginning, this may be easier said than done. However, as you proceed through the treatment, you are likely to view your success with pride and glory, and you will be very motivated to keep things clean. There is a small chance that this will not happen right away for you. In either case, you must find alternate places to store possessions besides the cleaned target areas.

If for some reason an item does find its way into any of the previously cleaned target areas, you must remove the item before moving on to any new target areas. Remember that the actual cleaning process is only half of the work; the other half is maintaining the progress you've made. The only way to maintain the progress you've made is to continue to keep those target areas cleaned.

Regain Functional Use of the Space Created

The next step is to enjoy the results of your hard work. Use the space you have created in some functional way. For instance, if you just cleaned one-third of the kitchen table, then eat your meals there. If you cleaned off a recliner or a portion of a sofa, then use that space to rest, read, or strategize your next target area to clean.

The more you use the cleaned spaces for their intended purposes, the more you will want to maintain those areas. For instance, let's say that prior to cleaning, you had no place to sit down to watch television. You then successfully cleaned your recliner and enjoyed the benefits of your hard work by relaxing there often. The more you enjoy using the recliner, the more motivated you will be to keep it functional.

Step Five: Target a New Area

After successfully cleaning the first target area, you may move on to the next area. Remember, if your first target area was a fraction of a larger project, then your next target area is the next fraction of that same project. For example, if you successfully cleaned one-third of the kitchen table yesterday, then your next target area is the next third of the table. Or, if you cleaned one-half of the sofa, then the next area is the remaining half.

You may feel tempted to stray from an incomplete project and move on to another area. This is an urge that you must resist. It is extremely important for you to complete an entire target area before proceeding to a new one. Remember how good it felt to see the first third of the table completed? Seeing the second third will feel even better.

Adding the Maintenance Step

The first treatment session will be unique in that there are no previously cleaned target areas to maintain. For every subsequent cleaning session, you will begin by taking a few minutes to maintain your previously cleaned target areas. Scan the cleaned areas for items that don't belong, and put them away. Be careful not to get distracted—remember, you are not a highway construction worker.

Exercise: Begin the Treatment Program

Now that you have read this entire chapter, you are ready to begin the actual cleaning process. Follow the steps we have provided in the order listed:

1. Select the target area.

2. Assess items in the target area.

3. Use the three-and-a-half-box technique.

4. Maintain the cleaned target area.

5. Target a new area.

For every project you do after the first one, you will add the preliminary step of maintaining all previously cleaned target areas.

Good luck with your cleaning! Remember that the system may seem a little foreign to you, but that is probably good. New skills take getting used to before they become comfortable routines.

7

Continuing the Cleaning Program

Don't put off for tomorrow what you can do today, because if you enjoy it today you can do it again tomorrow.

—James A. Michener

By now you have successfully targeted and cleaned some areas in your home. Congratulations! You are beginning to see your hard work paying off, and you have more space to move around and enjoy your home.

In chapter 6 we encouraged you to begin the cleaning process in highly visible areas. The idea was to give you the immediate gratification and satisfaction that would help motivate you to successfully clean other areas. The first section of this chapter will outline how to target and clean the areas that are less visible but equally important.

Then we will talk about putting your possessions away and give you some organizational strategies as well.

Exercise: Assess How You're Doing

Take out your notebook and turn to a fresh page. Write down your thoughts and feelings about how you are doing in your treatment so far. Is it progressing as you thought it would? Are you surprised or not surprised by the treatment? Why? Are you feeling more motivated after clearing out some large, highly visible areas?

Next, write down some of your concerns about proceeding. Maybe you think you have done enough work, or maybe you think you have more important things to attend to. Perhaps you are upset that others do not appreciate how much you have accomplished, or maybe you are concerned about whether you can maintain the gains you have made. If you have these thoughts or similar ones, you need to address them now. Use your cognitive therapy strategies to break down these thoughts before going further.

Targeting the Less Visible Areas

Once you have cleaned and maintained larger spaces and furniture, it is important to begin targeting less visible areas like closets, dressers, storage cabinets, desk drawers, smaller tables, medicine cabinets, file cabinets, bookshelves, kitchen drawers, and underneath furniture.

Don't feel bad if you are afraid to tackle these areas. Many hoarders fill these smaller, out-of-sight storage spaces beyond their intended capacity, so they can be very overwhelming to address. It is very common for areas like drawers and closets to be filled with so much clutter that opening and closing them requires agility.

In fact, many hoarders have closets stuffed to the brim with possessions. People are often afraid to open closet doors because they may be ambushed by falling possessions, which can be dangerous, especially if some of the items are large and heavy, like bowling balls, skis, or books. If your closets are completely full, you may want to wear a helmet and padding when opening closet doors.

On the other hand, your closets and drawers may be completely empty. Perhaps you have been hesitant to decide what goes where, or you told yourself you would organize your possessions and put them into drawers and closets later, but later never came.

Continue to Use the Three-and-a-Half-Box Technique

No matter what condition your less visible spaces are in, you need to filter out the items you want to save from those you want to discard. Remember, your goal remains the same as in chapter 6: you are to throw away possessions you do not need and save the ones you do. Later on, you will decide where the saved possessions will go.

You will use the same treatment steps we outlined in chapter 6 for the remaining target areas. Use the same scheduling approach, the same motivational strategies, and the same cognitive therapy techniques as you did with the larger, more visible areas.

You may feel tempted to stray from the treatment program while targeting these less visible areas. For example, let's say that when you are cleaning out a closet, you find a long-lost favorite pair of shoes, and you want to put them in the bedroom so you don't forget about them later. You need to resist that urge! Putting the shoes in a different room is simply moving the clutter from one area to another. Fight that urge and put them in the Save box.

Try to break down each less visible target area into several manageable projects. For instance, if there are six drawers in your dresser, then identify each drawer as its own target area. If each drawer looks like it could be broken down into smaller projects, don't hesitate to do so. This way you will be much more productive and feel better about yourself than if you targeted too much at once and got frustrated in the process.

Remember to Maintain All Previously Cleaned Areas

It is likely that you will use a previously cleaned area in the process of cleaning a less visible target area. For example, let's say that you are targeting one of the kitchen drawers now. You may take out the items in that drawer and put them on the already cleaned kitchen table to make them more accessible during the cleaning process. This is okay as long as you completely clean off the table and leave it clean when you are finished with the kitchen drawer. Be sure to give yourself enough time to complete each target area so that you do not have to leave a partially completed area unattended for a long period of time. If you lose focus or lack motivation to complete the project after a long break, it may become new clutter. It is especially important that you always keep your functional living spaces clear. We'll talk more about relapse prevention in chapter 8.

Keep Using the Display Box

It is fairly common for people to forget about the Display box while cleaning less visible areas, especially closets and drawers. Some of the possessions you find in the closets, drawers, and cabinets you're cleaning will eventually be permanently stored in the places you found them. For instance, let's say you live in a single-family home in a city where it snows during the winter. While cleaning out the front closet, you come across snow boots, shovels, and other winter accessories. You feel (perhaps rightly so) that these possessions should remain in this closet, so you keep them in a corner of the closet while sorting other possessions. You just strayed from the treatment a little and did one of those I'll-just-keep-it-here-for-now moves. It is good that you decided the items would be stored in the closet, but remember that your current goal is to remove all possessions from the target area and make specific decisions about which box they belong in. If you think some possessions belong permanently in the target area, remove them and place them in the Display box. When the target area is cleaned, you will remove the items from the box and put them back where they belong.

It may not be obvious to you what the less visible areas will store when the cleaning process is completed. You may have to determine how you will use these particular areas prior to cleaning them. You need to decide before you start you cleaning so you know what to put in the Display box. In the more visible areas, that decision is easier. You know what a kitchen table, sofa, or bed is used for, but you will need to decide how each kitchen drawer will be used.

We will address this issue in more detail later in this chapter, when we discuss how to put your possessions away. Right now, you do not need to know exactly what will go in each target area, but you should have a general idea.

Protecting Your Health While You Clean

As you progress through the cleaning of your home, especially the less visible areas, you may find yourself sneezing, coughing, and having headaches. In fact, you may uncover answers to some of your unexplained chronic ailments. In chapter 3 we mentioned that in our experience, hoarders are more likely than nonhoarders to have headaches, respiratory problems like asthma and coughing, allergies, fatigue, lethargy, and sleeping difficulties.

Two of the biggest culprits are dust and dirt. In the cleanup of your home, you will undoubtedly find dust and dirt (among other things) on the surfaces underneath and around your clutter. In fact, don't be surprised if while cleaning you endure some physical discomfort. Moving possessions around causes dust to rise into the air and may trigger headaches or allergies.

These physical conditions can disrupt your ability to follow through with the treatment program. For example, if you develop a headache because of the dust in the target area, you may lose your focus and possibly get distracted. Additionally, the headache may cause you to feel depressed or dejected about how long it has been since you cleaned that area, and you may feel less motivated to finish the project.

Here are some suggestions to help you cope with the dust and dirt.

- While cleaning, try to have as many windows open as possible.

- Vacuum newly uncovered floor space immediately. Do not wait to vacuum the entire room at once. There are two reasons for this. First, dangerous items like tacks, pins, staples, or broken glass may become exposed when you remove clutter. The more quickly they are removed, the less risk there is for injuries. Second, you will get more positive visual reinforcement from seeing a vacuumed floor.

- Use cleaning supplies to remove dust and dirt from shelves, cabinets, drawers, and other less visible storage areas. Again, do not wait until the whole area is cleaned.

- For areas you know will be very dusty, use a mask to cover your nose and mouth during the cleanup.

- Wash your hands thoroughly after each target area is cleaned. This will help prevent the spread of airborne or foodborne illnesses.

Exercise: Identify Less Visible Target Areas

Now that you have some larger areas and furniture cleared, take out your notebook and identify the less visible areas you would like to target. Then begin clearing the clutter in these areas, using the same process you did with the larger areas. Schedule times for cleaning, and don't forget to reward yourself. It is very important that you stay with one target area at a time. Do not stray from one area to another, and remember to break down target areas into several smaller, more manageable projects. When you have a system that works, stay with it. Good luck!

Troubleshooting Ideas to Help You Deal with Indecision

We certainly understand that the cleaning process can be quite difficult at times and would like to give you a few suggestions to help make it easier. If you are having difficulty deciding whether to keep certain possessions, or if your Save boxes are growing uncontrollably, these suggestions will help.

What to Do with Old Clothes

Old clothes can occupy a significant amount of functional storage space, so making decisions about clothing is very important. We have found that hoarders tend to hold on to old clothes for a variety of reasons. Below are some of those reasons and suggestions about how to address the issues.

Keeping Clothes Just in Case You Wear Them Again

When it comes to clothes, many people have difficulty making decisions, even nonhoarders. Here are a few things to keep in mind.

First, consider the *75-25 rule*: Most people wear 25 percent of their clothes about 75 percent of the time. Think about it for yourself. Does it seem to apply? Look at some of the people closest to you. Do they really take full advantage of every article in their wardrobe and wear something completely different every day, or do they seem to recycle the same outfits throughout the weeks? The answer is probably closer to the latter.

Now ask yourself how much you really need the clothes you just discovered in the closet. Do you really wear all of them? Do you really need them? This is a good opportunity to use your cognitive therapy techniques. Technically, you don't really need anything but food, water, and shelter in order to survive. So maybe a healthier question to ask yourself is whether you really want these newly found clothes in your closet, or can you get by without them?

To help with this question, ask yourself whether you have worn the item in the last year. If not, you are better off discarding it. If you are thinking that maybe you'll hold on to it in case that style comes back in the future, remember that although it may come back, the new retro look will likely be trendier than your older saved version.

Furthermore, if you keep the item for another ten to fifteen years waiting for the style to return, it is occupying valuable closet space where you could store the clothes you actually wear 75 percent of the time. Ironic, isn't it, that you store the just-in-case clothes in the closet and have the clothes you actually wear stored on furniture or in clutter around the house.

Of the clothing you have kept in the past in case the style returned, how many items have you worn again? Did you actually take out your bell-bottom pants from the 1970s when they made a comeback in the late 1990s?

If you have never (or rarely) worn something later that you held on to "just in case," then chances are you will find this to be true in the future, too. If you have not worn something in one year or more, you are better off discarding or donating it.

Holding On to Clothes Until You Give Them Away

Perhaps you are holding on to your old clothes because you intend to give them to a relative or a charity. Maybe you have promised to give your children's old clothes to a sibling or a neighbor. In fact, you may have very good intentions for the old clothes you're hanging on to, but just haven't gotten around to following through with those intentions. Perhaps you feel guilty about donating the clothes to a charity because you promised them to someone you know.

Although you may have had a plan of action for the old clothes, it is likely that months or years have passed and the clothes are still hanging in your closets or piled on your floor. Sometimes hoarders will buy new clothes and save them with the intention of giving them later as gifts. However, the majority of those future presents never make it out of the closet.

Ask yourself how often you have actually retrieved an item from your closet and given it to someone as a present. Even if you have done it a few times, does it justify keeping the items and subjecting yourself and your family to the resulting clutter? We suggest that you place all clothes that have not been used in the past year in the Discard/Recycle box. Later on, you can donate them either to a charity or to a specific person. Remember, your current goal is to uncover and reclaim functional storage space for the clothes you actually wear so they don't remain as clutter.

Holding on to Clothes Until You Have Them Cleaned

Perhaps you wanted to give your old clothes away but never got around to it because you just did not have the time to wash, iron, or dry-clean them. We suggest you give your possessions away in their current condition. If they are badly stained, ripped, or not wearable, put them into a garbage bag now. Clothing that is wearable goes straight into the Discard/Recycle box to be given away as is.

Think about department stores that sell clothing as is on the clearance racks. If a department store can sell you clothes without laundering, dry-cleaning, or repairing them, why is it that you have to wash old clothes before giving them away?

If you are concerned about what others will think of you if you give away unwashed clothes, you need to address these thoughts with your cognitive therapy strategies. Where is the evidence that you will be criticized for giving away clothes without laundering them first? Why do you need everyone's approval? Where is it written that someone will not appreciate clothes that are not washed as much as they would appreciate washed clothes?

Magazines, Newspapers, and Loose Papers

These items usually represent a large percentage of clutter within the homes of hoarders. Take a look around your home. Do you have large numbers of these items? If so, why did you keep them? If you believe that not reading the magazines and newspapers means you are stupid or ignorant, go back to chapter 5 and make yourself a cognitive therapy flash card now. It is important that you challenge this belief and develop a more rational response before attempting to make decisions about discarding these items.

If that thought does not apply to you, or if you have successfully developed a rational response but are still having difficulty deciding whether to keep or discard these items, don't worry. Here are a few suggestions.

First, most written material becomes outdated quickly. Newspapers become outdated within a few days because they are written daily. The stories are updated constantly, making earlier reports obsolete. Further, the same information is available through television and radio news programs. Magazines become outdated within five to seven months, sometimes even sooner.

For this reason, we suggest you follow the *six-month rule* for written material: If a magazine was printed six or more months ago, you should probably recycle or discard it. Obviously, there are exceptions to the rule, like a newspaper that features a story about something dear to you. But generally speaking, the newspapers and magazines are occupying valuable functional living space.

Keep in mind that there are other ways to retrieve the same information contained in the newspapers and magazines that cover your floors. For example, you can find most (if not all) of the printed information on the Internet. We call this *accessing it elsewhere*. Most major magazines and newspapers have Web sites where you can access the same articles and stories found in the printed versions. Also, many magazines and newspapers can be found at your local library if you really want to see the printed version of an article. Knowing that there are alternate sources for the information you feel is important can sometimes make it easier to decide to discard or recycle written materials.

If you plan to keep magazines or newspapers until you get around to cutting articles out and filing them, chances are it will never happen. Think about the last time you cut out an article, filed it away, and actually went back to read it. Even if you have gone back to some articles, was it worth the aggravation of keeping piles of papers around, having a messy home and a family who is upset with you, all the while knowing you could have accessed the information elsewhere?

Perhaps you think it is easier to have the information available rather than trying to seek it out. Is that really accurate? Isn't it in fact easier to look something up on the Internet or go to a local library for help than to sort through tons of newspapers and magazines in the hope of finding the information? Even if you had the perfect filing system, it would be extremely time-consuming to find the precise information you were looking for.

It is better at the beginning to go to an extreme and discard all magazines and newspapers until your hoarding behaviors are under better control. Then, if you can throw out newspapers daily, there will be no need to keep them around for six months. Use the six-month rule only for the written materials you have in your possession now.

Plastic and Paper Bags

You have probably found lots of paper and plastic bags throughout your cleaning. Don't feel bad; it's very common for hoarders to hold on to these items "just in case" a need arises for them in the future. However, you have probably saved significantly more bags than you need. You may have thought at the time that there would be a need for a particular bag or bags, but apparently that need has not yet arisen. If anything, these bags are taking up valuable storage room and preventing you from storing the things you actually use.

You may want to pick out the bags that are in the best condition and save those. Or you may want to keep a few old bags for utility purposes plus a few nicer ones for special occasions. Whatever you do, try to limit the number of bags you decide to save.

One helpful technique is to use what we call the *stuff-in rule*: The number of bags you can stuff into one bag of that type is the number you can keep. However, you need to be able to tie the storage bag without difficulty. Usually, you can stuff about fifteen plastic grocery bags into one empty bag and successfully tie it off. You can fit between five and ten paper bags inside a single bag, depending on their size. The stuff-in rule means you'll have a sufficient number of bags on hand if a need arises in the future. Be sure to place the kept bags in the appropriate treatment box.

What to Do with Multiples of Things

You may also find yourself having difficulty deciding what to do with multiples of the same item. There are quite a few sources of multiples, including incoming mail, brochures, flyers, and bulletins. No matter how you acquired these multiples, you need to discard some (if not most) of them. In the next chapter, we will discuss techniques for reducing the acquisition of new possessions, including multiples.

Generally speaking, a good method for reducing the volume of items in your home is to allot a maximum of one backup for every original version. For highly sensitive items, you may allot up to two backups, but this should be the exception, not the rule. For example, let's say that you find several copies of the flyer you made for your daughter's school play, and it has a special meaning in your heart. In this case, it would be acceptable to keep one or two copies and discard the rest. But the next items you find in your cleaning are several copies of an invitation to a church function that happened over seven years ago. You missed the function and the invitations have no special meaning to you, so here it would be wise to discard all of them.

This policy of keeping a reasonable number of backups also applies to pens, pencils, and erasers. You may find literally hundreds of these items throughout your cleaning. Many hoarders do not realize they have an excessive number of pens and pencils because they are scattered throughout the clutter. You or your spouse may then purchase more supplies or pick up extras from work because it's difficult to find them in the clutter at home. We suggest that you keep a total of five pens or pencils on your desk and another five in the kitchen or by the phone.

A helpful technique for deciding which writing materials to keep is to test their functionality. When you come across a pen or pencil, test the ink or eraser. If the pen is out of ink, discard it, and if the eraser is rock hard and doesn't erase, discard the pencil.

If you currently acquire things in multiples, stop immediately. Unless you are going to use several items right away, just purchase one. There is no need to buy several vases, pans, or bottles of ketchup unless you have a need for those multiples right now. You are not making your life easier by buying everything at once. In fact, your attempts at making your life easier have actually made your life more complicated and certainly more cluttered. If you find it very difficult to resist purchasing multiples, make yourself a cognitive therapy flash card and carry it with you when you go shopping.

Here's a summary of the strategies we recommend for less visible areas:

Written materials

- recycle
- six-month rule
- access it elsewhere

Paper or plastic bags

- stuff-in rule

Clothing

- 75-25 rule
- one-year ownership plan
- donate or sell

Multiples

- allot one or two backups
- test functionality of multiples

Deciding When to Stop Cleaning and Begin Organizing

We generally recommend that you end the cleaning treatment when the entire home is cleaned, although we would support the decision to end the cleaning process when you have successfully finished at least 80 percent of the areas you wanted to clean. Your decision will depend on your situation.

If you have significant family pressure to regain functional living space, or if you do not have enough time to dedicate to the cleaning process to clean the entire home, you may want to clean only highly functional rooms like the kitchen and organize the possessions in those rooms as quickly as possible. You may feel okay about waiting to clean less functional areas of the home like the spare bedroom.

On the other hand, you may have more time to dedicate to the cleaning or have less intense pressure from your family. If this is the case, you may want to clean the entire home before organizing your possessions.

There is no right or wrong answer here. You have to make the decision that is the best for you. If you decide to begin the organizational process before you have cleaned the entire home, keep the following things in mind:

- Make sure you have ample storage space for the possessions to be organized. Have enough closet or drawer space to put things away. Do not partially clean closets or drawers. You need to be certain that organized items will not be combined with unsorted clutter.

- Have a clear understanding of the project you are working on. Stay with one project at a time. Remember that you are not a highway construction worker. While you are organizing your possessions and putting them back where they belong, do not get sidetracked and start to discard garbage or clutter.

- Make sure there is a clear distinction between areas that have been cleaned and those that have clutter.

Putting Stuff Away

The remainder of this chapter outlines the organizational process for you. At the end of this chapter is an exercise that will help you actually begin the organizational process. Be sure to read all the way through the end of the chapter before you begin to put things away.

Now that you have ended the cleaning part of the treatment, you are ready to organize your possessions and put them where they belong. Before you begin this part of the treatment, congratulate yourself for your accomplishments thus far! You have come a long way. Remember that *you* did this work and *you* made the decisions about what to keep and what to discard, so *you* deserve the credit! Try to take that same focus you had during the cleanup and bring it into the reorganization phase of the treatment.

Go Back to the Save Boxes

Back in chapter 6, you signed your name and agreed to not retrieve things from the Save boxes. Well, that agreement no longer applies. Now is the time to go back to those boxes and put away the possessions you decided to keep.

However, putting stuff away will not be a chaotic, random activity. It will be as structured and systematic as the cleanup part of the treatment was. Remember that it was structure that got you this far, so don't start a new style now. Stay with what you know works.

Figure Out What Goes Where

One of the most important steps you need to take before putting things away is to designate the places where items will be stored. You may already have a general idea of this from our discussion earlier in this chapter about knowing what the Display box would contain. However, now you need a more detailed plan.

Keep in mind that you built up clutter prior to the treatment because you could not find an appropriate place for each item, or because you decided to "just put it here for now and figure it out later," but later never came. In a sense, later is now. Now is the time to find an appropriate place for your possessions.

The following lists will help give you a better sense of what kinds of items people generally keep in different storage areas. Keep in mind that some items could be stored in more than one area, so items may be listed in more than one place. These lists are just a suggestion, and if you feel that your possessions could be placed elsewhere, that is fine. However, you do need to make a decision about how to use each of your storage areas.

Exercise: Identify What Will Go Where

Take out your notebook, and on a fresh page, make a column for each of the storage areas you have (or as many as you can think of). Then, in each column, list the types of items you think should go in that area. Try to be specific so you can refer to this exercise when you're actually putting things away.

You may feel this is too simplistic, and you may in fact feel silly doing this task. You may think it is somehow demeaning. Just remember that the task of cleaning up clutter can be overwhelming and we are giving you strategies to reduce your anxiety.

Desk Drawers	Kitchen Cabinets	Storage Closets
pens and pencils	food	boxes
rubber bands	dishes	sporting goods
paper clips	pots and pans	suitcases
calculator	cookbooks	cleaning supplies
stapler	appliances	extra toilet paper
computer disks	paper and plastic	and paper towels
important personal	bags	out-of-season
items	**Bedroom Closets**	clothing
working files and	clothing	memorabilia
active papers	personal effects	**Linen Closet**
receipts	shoes	towels
Bookcases	purses and bags	linens
books	**Dresser Drawers**	guest supplies
magazines	clothing	blankets
pictures	**Nightstands**	**Front Closet**
knickknacks	actively read books	active jackets and
music	and magazines	coats
Kitchen Drawers	frequently used	active clothes (shoes
silverware	medicines	and bags)
utensils	pictures or	umbrellas
recipes	memorabilia	sporting goods
pot holders	**Under the Bed**	**Bathroom Cabinet**
pens and pencils	storage boxes	cleaning supplies
coupons	containing clothes or	extra toilet paper
sponges	blankets	toiletries
Armoires/TV Stands	**Hutches**	hair dryer
television	pictures	**Medicine Chest**
video games	memorabilia	toiletries
music	collectibles	medicine
movies	dishes	Band-Aids

Use the One-by-One Rule

After you have read the rest of this chapter, you will be ready to organize your possessions throughout your home. How will you do this? Again, keep in mind that the organizational part of the treatment will follow the same type of structure as the cleanup.

We strongly encourage you to use the *one-by-one rule.* You must go through the Save boxes *one box at a time.* When you are ready to begin organizing, go to the area where you have kept the Save boxes and choose one box. Once you have chosen the box, take *one item at a time* out of the box. This way you will stay focused on the task at hand and avoid getting overwhelmed and frustrated.

You can think of the one-by-one rule as being similar to the way you successfully addressed each target area during the cleanup. This systematic approach will be a major asset to you during the organizational phase of treatment. If you tried to put away many items at once, you would likely lose sight of your goal and allow clutter to form again.

You may be saying to yourself that putting things away one at a time could take forever. Keep in mind that you got to this point by deciding the fate of your possessions one at a time, and that did not take forever; in fact it was quite successful. Remember that new strategies usually feel foreign at first. The more practice you get, the more comfortable you will become. As you get more comfortable with this strategy, you will be able to proceed at a faster pace.

As you remove each item from the box, decide where that item belongs. You may need to refer to the lists we provided or the ones you created in the last exercise. Once you have decided where that item belongs, go ahead and place it there. Then return to the box and pick up the next item.

Only after you have removed all of the items from that Save box can you start removing items from a new box. Be sure to continue with this strategy for all the remaining Save boxes.

Keep Some Discard/Recycle Boxes Nearby

As you put away the items in the Save boxes, you may find yourself wondering why you decided to keep some of the items, especially those in the first few Save boxes you created during the cleanup program. This is very common. Remember that in the beginning, your decision-making skills were probably not as strong as they are now. In fact, it is very unlikely that you will wish to keep all the items from your first Save boxes.

If you find some items that you no longer wish to keep, you may decide to discard, recycle, or donate them. Be sure to follow the same system of deciding what to do with one item at a time.

Items Do Not Need the Perfect Final Resting Place

If you are having difficulty deciding where to put some items because you can't find the "perfect" place for them, you should temporarily stop organizing your items and take out your cognitive therapy flash cards or create some new cards now.

Remember that waiting to find the perfect place for your possessions got you into this mess in the first place, and continuing to look for that perfect place will only lead to more frustration. Review the cognitive therapy steps from chapter 5 and challenge your beliefs about the perfect placement of items. You may be engaging in all-or-nothing thinking or making should statements.

A more rational response might sound like *I may feel temporarily uncomfortable putting this item in an imperfect place, but I will be better able to enjoy my home and possessions if I choose to put this away anyway.*

Address the Empty Save Boxes and the Items to Be Sold or Donated

As you progress through the Save boxes, you will begin to see the number of those boxes diminish, and you will begin to feel more confident and proud of yourself. When you have completely emptied a Save box, you have two options. First, you can save *a few* of those boxes for use in the future. If you save all the boxes, you will just be establishing new clutter. Designate a storage site for these boxes, and put them there. The other option is simply to discard them all. There is no right or wrong choice here, but you do need to make a choice.

Items to be donated can be dropped off at a local charity or donation center. If you wish to make a tax-deductible donation, then you will need to make a list of the types of items donated and have a sense of each item's individual worth. Many donation centers offer guidelines about the value of commonly donated items. A general rule of thumb is that used items are worth about one-third of their retail price. Some donation centers will come to your home to pick up the items.

Finally, you need to address the items you plan to sell. If you have enough of these items, you may wish to have a garage sale. If you feel there are not enough items to have a sale, you may want to consider donating the items, taking them to a consignment shop, or possibly hosting a joint garage sale with a friend or neighbor.

If you have a garage sale, you may be able to make a little cash (or a lot of cash) for all your hard work removing clutter from your home. This is a nice way to celebrate the culmination of days, weeks, or months of hard work. You can set whatever prices you feel are reasonable. Again, one-third of retail price is a good place to start. To help bring in more potential customers, you may wish to advertise the sale with flyers or an ad in a local newspaper.

Exercise: Begin Putting Stuff Away

Now you are ready to begin the second half of your treatment program. It's time to start putting your possessions away. Go ahead and choose the first Save box to unpack and put away. Remember these strategies for success:

- Schedule blocks of time for organizing.
- Stay on task and focus on one project at a time. Remember that you are not a highway construction worker!
- Decide generally what storage areas will store.
- Use the one-by-one rule: Work on only one box at a time, and take out only one item at a time.
- Keep Discard and Recycle boxes nearby.
- Make cognitive therapy flash cards if necessary.

8

Enjoying Your Home and Preventing Relapse

People often say that this or that person has not yet found himself. But the self is not something that one finds. It is something one creates.

—Thomas Szasz

Congratulations! You have successfully cleaned and organized the clutter in your home. How does it feel? We hope you are very proud of yourself. However, it would be understandable if you were skeptical about your ability to keep your home orderly over the long run. This chapter is designed to help you maintain the gains you have made and cut down the number of items coming into your home.

Maintain All Previously Cleaned Areas

This is something we have stated many times throughout this book, because it is a tremendously important issue. The best way to maintain the gains you have made is to keep all cleaned areas clean. Be realistic in your thoughts and expectations about the future. You will have things (mail, purchases, subscriptions, and so on) constantly coming into your home, creating the opportunity for you to go back to old, unhealthy habits that create clutter. But you *can* handle those items and you *can* maintain the wonderful progress you have made. The following sections will give you some skills and techniques to help you do just that.

Set Daily and Weekly Cleaning Goals

In order to keep clutter from building up again, you will need to clean your home more often. Ideally, you will be able to do a little cleaning every day, or most of the cleaning within a week. Again, any skepticism you may have about the likelihood of following through with this is understandable. Many people doubt that they can become consistent cleaners.

But remember, you also had some reservations about your ability to clean up your clutter, and look where you are now! A little concern about cleaning is reasonable, but if you have severe doubts, you may want to create a few cognitive therapy flash cards now to help you out. You can do this.

Below is a good outline of the types of cleaning activities you should be doing weekly, monthly, and twice a year. Initially, it may seem like a lot of cleaning, but try to look at this table the same way you looked at large target areas during the cleanup part of the treatment. Break down the weekly cleaning goals into smaller, more manageable projects. Try doing at least one of the six projects every day.

Unless you live in a mansion or palace and there are thirty or more rooms to clean, none of these six projects should take very long, especially taking out the garbage and recycling. Even the dusting and mopping should require less than an hour each. If you can get into the routine of doing one or more of these activities each day, maintaining your clutter-free home will be a piece of cake.

Weekly

- vacuum rugs and carpets

- dust furniture and blinds (use duster and spray cleaner)

- clean and disinfect bathrooms and kitchen (toilets, bathtub, shower, sinks)

- mop floors

- take out garbage

- take out recycling

Monthly

- wash windows (using ammonia-based spray cleaner)

- clean out refrigerator (throw out expired items; if you're not sure of the expiration date, throw it out anyway)

- throw out old bills and mail

- clean filters in air conditioners and heaters

Twice a year

- clean and dust behind refrigerator

- check batteries in fire alarms, carbon monoxide alarms, and flashlights

- inspect gauge on fire extinguisher

- change vacuum cleaner filter

- clean under beds and flip mattresses

Exercise: Create a Daily and Weekly Chart for Cleaning

Take out your notebook and find three fresh pages. Copy the table below on each of the three pages. On the first page, label it *Table A: Weekly Cleaning.* On the second page, label it *Table B: Monthly Cleaning.* On the third page, label it *Table C: Twice-Yearly Cleaning.* Then tear out all three pages from your notebook. Photocopy table A twenty-four times, and photocopy table B six times.

Arrange the photocopies in the following order. Take four copies of table A, then put one copy of table B under those copies. Take another four copies of table A and under those put a copy of table B. Follow this process until you are out of tables A and B. Put the one page of table C underneath the last table B.

You now have enough cleaning charts to get you through six months. If this program is successful for you, make more copies in six months. Using the lists of weekly, monthly, and twice-yearly cleaning tasks as a reference guide, go ahead and identify what tasks you'd like to perform on each day. Notice that there are only six weekly activities, so you will have one day a week off. If you can think of other tasks you want to add, go ahead. When you get to the monthly and twice-yearly items, fill in the tasks you would like to do each day.

Starting today, proceed with the cleaning. If you'd like to try doing more than one activity per day, go ahead. If that works, continue it; if not, go back to one task per day. After you have performed the activity, check it off in the Done column and be proud of yourself. Good luck!

Day	Activity	Done
Monday		
Tuesday		
Wednesday		
Thursday		
Friday		
Saturday		
Sunday		

Enjoy Your Home

Now that you have a more functional home, you may want to take advantage of this and invite people over for parties or meals. By inviting others over, you put a little pressure on yourself to maintain the wonderful gains you have made. Additionally, having people over will increase your confidence and self-esteem, thus increasing your motivation to keep your house free of clutter.

Try inviting a friend or relative over for coffee or for a meal. If you can set up visits within a few weeks, this will give people enough time to fit the plans into their schedule, and will also give you enough time to put a little pressure on yourself to stay on top of the cleaning. Use the skills and techniques in this chapter *before* your guests arrive.

Try to make this a regular process. Invite the same guests again, or try inviting other guests to your home. The more often people are in your home, the more motivated you will be to maintain a clutter-free home.

Another benefit of inviting others to your home is that they become tuned in to your desire to be with them and may invite you out more often than they did before. This will also improve your overall confidence and self-esteem.

Make Home Homier

You may find yourself looking around your cleaner and more functional home thinking that it does not feel cozy or welcoming. This is very common. For many hoarders, clutter often causes the home to feel devoid of color, warmth, and charm.

Perhaps throughout the years you have found yourself saying that you'll get to decorating your home later, after you've finished cleaning, or that decorating does not make a difference if clutter is everywhere. In some ways, you may have become used to seeing the clutter around, and although it caused a variety of negative emotions, it served as your home's primary—or only—décor.

Clutter may have physically prevented you from decorating your home. For example, you may have a completely bare wall because your clutter made it impossible for you to get to the wall to put up paintings. Or maybe you would have liked to decorate the dining room hutch with photographs of your family but could not find enough space in the hutch to put the pictures.

The more you view clutter as décor, the more depressed and isolated you are likely to feel. Keep in mind that part of the reason you were successful in cleaning your clutter was that you targeted areas that provided you with positive visual reinforcement. Allowing clutter to serve as décor creates negative visual reinforcement. When you removed the clutter and saw the contrast between the clutter and cleanliness, you not only increased your motivation to clean again but also increased your confidence.

Now that you are rid of your clutter, you may also be rid of your home's sole source of décor. This is a good time to create a warmer and more inviting home filled with décor that inspires and motivates you. Here are some suggestions to help make your home homier.

- Put fresh flowers on tabletops.

- Put knickknacks in bookcases, hutches, or other display cases.

- Have a mixture of tall and short plants. (You can use artificial plants also.)

- Place photographs of friends and family members throughout your home.

- Hang photographs, paintings, or posters on the walls.

- Hang mirrors on the walls. This will create the sense of added space.

- Display one or two coffee-table books on tabletops.

- Use area carpets on hardwood floors. This helps to bring in different colors.

- If you paint or wallpaper walls, try to use warm colors.

Exercise: Identify Your Home's New Décor

Take out your notebook and find a fresh page. List all the rooms in your home that you would like to decorate, and after each room, leave some space to write your decorating ideas. Be as specific as you can, because you will come back to this exercise later in this chapter.

Stay in the Moment: Accept Responsibilities as They Come

Now that you have started to maintain your treatment gains, it is time to discuss other strategies to help prevent relapses in the future. The strategies outlined in the next few sections will help you fight your tendency to put off for tomorrow what could be done today.

We certainly understand that establishing new patterns of behavior can be very difficult. However, we have confidence in you, and we think you can do much more than you have believed yourself able to do in the past. Just look at how much progress you have already made. Remember, clutter is the enemy!

Eliminate the Here-for-Now Mentality

Perhaps you tend to just put items "here for now." This is a large contributor to the development and maintenance of clutter. You may believe that just putting one item "here for now" won't make a difference. This would be true if you were only talking about one item; however, if you just spent weeks or months cleaning clutter, chances are you probably did it for *every* item coming into your home.

This is exactly why we need to give you some skills and strategies to help you do things in the moment rather than putting them off for the future. You may be thinking that putting things away immediately as they come into your home will be too difficult or not worth the time, or that you should be able to relax before you put things away, or you may have some other excuse as to why you can't or shouldn't do it now.

Hopefully you picked up on the should statements in the last sentence. If you recognize yourself in the examples we gave, you might want to take out those cognitive therapy flash cards and review them or make new cards regarding your concerns.

Here is something to keep in mind when making those flash cards. Although the strategies we're going to teach you may seem uncomfortable and new, they will only take minutes per day. This is in contrast to the days, weeks, or months that you just spent cleaning up all the clutter that you just put "here for now."

We have created four strategies to help you eliminate your here-for-now mentality. If you use these strategies, you can "play it SAFE" and prevent relapses in the future.

Store new items immediately.

Assign functionality to areas.

Filter incoming mail and other papers.

Employ the weekend-basket technique.

Store New Items Immediately

The first strategy in SAFE is to immediately put away items that enter your home. These items may include recent purchases, free materials you picked up, dry cleaning, books, and so on. In chapter 7 we discussed the importance of deciding what types of possessions you would store in each of your home's storage areas. Now that you know what goes where, it's time to get in the habit of putting things where they belong right away.

For example, let's say that you have just come home from a day of shopping and errands. In your hands, you have a bag of newly purchased clothes, picture frames, home office supplies, and some soda. Instead of putting everything down "here for now," it would be healthier to store each of those items away in its appropriate place, then put your feet up and relax.

So you put the clothes in your bedroom closet, put the picture frames and home office supplies in the drawers of the desk in the den, and put the soda in the refrigerator. No matter how tired you are, the longest those things could possibly take would be three minutes. Remember, it's either those three minutes or the weeks and months in the future cleaning the clutter again. Think about how great you will feel after putting everything away and having maintained your beautiful home.

Assign Functionality to Areas

The second strategy in SAFE is to assign some boundaries about the types of activities you will do in each of the rooms in your home.

If you have ever tried to lose weight, you may have been advised to eat your meals only at the kitchen table or dining room table. If you eat your meals in front of the television or in bed, you may start to associate those areas with eating and feel hungry when in those areas. If you regularly eat in front of the television, you may actually feel hungry just because you are watching television, whereas if you were in another room doing something different, you would not feel hungry.

This phenomenon also contributes to insomnia or difficulty sleeping. One of the very first things that is addressed in treating insomnia is *sleep hygiene,* or the kinds of behaviors that you are engaging in around sleep time. For example, if you tend to watch television or read in bed, you may have difficulty falling asleep later on. This happens because your brain is confused about what the bed is supposed to be used for. If you use the bed only for sleeping and sexual activity, then you will have less insomnia.

How does this relate to hoarding? If you are using the kitchen table not only as a place to eat meals but also as a place to temporarily store items, you will forget what the table is supposed to be used for and will be more likely to develop clutter there. Or if you tend to pay your bills wherever you find them, not in one designated area, you are more likely to have bills all over the place, resulting in clutter. Instead, what you need to do is decide how each room in your home will be used and then stick to those boundaries.

Living Room	**Kitchen**	talk on phone
watch television	eat meals	try on clothes
entertain guests	entertain guests	get dressed
read books	read magazines and newspapers	**Den/Library**
exercise		pay bills
	organize calendar	read
Dining Room	**Bedroom**	organize calendar
entertain guests	sleep	talk on phone
eat formal meals	engage in sexual activity	use computer
eat casual meals		

Following are examples of how people use areas of their homes. You can see that some of the activities are listed in more than one area. This is because there are some activities you can do in several rooms, while other activities should be done in only one place.

Notice that we've listed the activities that you can do in each room. This is different from designating what each of the rooms will store.

Exercise: Assign Functions to Rooms in Your Home

In your notebook, identify the types of activities you will do in every room throughout your home. Obviously, you are not going to list everything you will do in the rooms but rather identify the main types of activities.

The more consistent you are in doing these activities in their designated rooms, the less likely you are to redevelop clutter in the future.

Filter Incoming Mail and Other Paper Goods

The third aspect of SAFE is to take care of incoming mail and paper goods effectively. This is an extremely important strategy in preventing clutter from forming, because incoming mail can consti-tute a large percentage of new items coming into your home. It's easy to slip into the here-for-now mentality with incoming mail, so you'll need to use our three-step plan instead.

Immediately throw away junk mail. The quicker you get rid of that junk mail, the better off you'll be. If you wait to discard it later, you may have instantly re-formed a clutter pile.

Separate remaining mail into four categories: active bills, things to do immediately, items to be filed away, and things to put on your calendar.

Put all sorted mail in a designated bill-paying location. Choose a good place to organize and pay the bills every month. Use an area like the desk in the den, or in a room where you can file active papers away.

Again, these steps may seem like a lot of work, but they should really take you no more than five to ten minutes per day. Would you rather spend a few minutes a day sorting incoming mail or spend weeks or months cleaning clutter? Keep in mind how good you will feel after choosing to keep your clutter under control and continuing to have a comfy, functional home.

Employ the Weekend-Basket Technique

The final step of SAFE is to use the *weekend-basket technique.* If you consistently use the other three steps of SAFE, this step becomes less necessary. However, if a few things slip through the cracks, or if you have family members who do not adhere to those steps, the weekend-basket technique will help you out tremendously in restoring order and preventing clutter.

All you need is a basket or a plastic container of some sort. The strategy has two steps, which need to be followed exactly:

1. Put all improperly placed items into the basket.

2. One at a time, transfer each item from the basket to its correct place.

As you can see, this strategy is not overly complicated, but it can be very difficult for some people to use correctly.

To use the weekend-basket strategy correctly, take the basket on a weekend day and roam around your home one room at a time. Think of it as a treasure hunt. You are on the lookout for any items not in their correct location. Pick up those items and place them in the basket. Continue this process in each room until you have gone through the entire home. If you have more items than will fit in your basket, get another basket. Only after you have gone through the entire home picking up inappropriately placed possessions will you return each item to its proper place.

Remember that you are not a highway construction worker. Your goal is to do one thing at a time and successfully finish each step. If you start doing two, three, four, or more things at once, you will get overwhelmed and lost, and clutter will accumulate again.

Try to notice how many items you pick up each week. Hopefully, the number of items will decrease over time, indicating that you are doing a better and better job of staying organized.

Create a Master Calendar

A great strategy in maintaining a well-run household and minimizing the buildup of clutter is to create and use a master calendar. We suggest that you use a large wall-sized calendar and either hang it or keep it on a desktop, whichever is easier for you. You can find a variety of calendars at office supply stores.

The calendar will help you remain updated on the family's events or simply your own. You need to decide if the calendar is yours or your family's. If you are having trouble deciding, you may be better off getting two calendars, one for yourself and the other for your family.

For every month, starting with the current month, write in important events and reminders. These may include

- family events (weddings, barbecues, and so on)

- birthdays and anniversaries

- work events (parties, conferences, and so on)

- reminders to pay the bills, due dates of bills

- kids' tests and homework deadlines

- reminders to file away items needing to be filed

- reminders and events from incoming mail

- guests' arrivals and departures

- social events (friends over for dinner, going out to movies, and so on)

If you think of events or other things to remember for future months, go ahead and put them in. Be sure to put the calendar in a place where it is highly visible. Also be sure to make all markings on the calendar very clear. You may wish to have other family members add their reminders to this calendar, or you may wish to have the calendar solely for your own events. There is no right or wrong way; do what you think is healthiest for you. Be certain to keep the calendar clutter-free. Remove any inappropriately placed clutter as soon as you notice it near the calendar.

Go back to the Identify Your Home's New Décor exercise earlier in this chapter, when we asked you to write down some decorating ideas for specific rooms in your home. Think about when you can do some of those projects, and mark them on the calendar also.

Limit the Number of New Items Entering Your Home

If you feel that acquiring new possessions is not an issue for you and that your main concern was cleaning up the clutter and maintaining your gains, then you may just want to skim through this section. However, if you have had great difficulty limiting the number of items you acquire, read through this section carefully.

In chapter 6 we discussed some basic strategies to help you limit the number of new items entering your home to increase the effectiveness of the cleanup. This section will address those issues in more detail by giving you some solid strategies and skills to help you maintain the results of the hard work you have done thus far.

Expose Yourself

We briefly introduced exposure with response prevention (E/RP) in our discussion of cognitive behavioral therapy, but we will go into further detail now. For many hoarders, acquiring new possessions is a compulsion that serves to relieve anxiety in the short term. You can use E/RP to strengthen your ability to resist acquiring new items.

E/RP is a technique whereby you place yourself in an anxiety-producing situation without engaging in any compulsions or acts to try to decrease the anxiety. E/RP is effective because of the process of habituation. To review, habituation is your body's natural ability to react with less and less anxiety the more you expose yourself to an anxiety-producing situation. As your body habituates to the situation, you become more confident in tolerating the anxiety without having to artificially decrease it by engaging in any compulsions.

There are two forms of E/RP: *imaginal* (using imagination and visualization) and *in vivo* (in real life). Both can be successful, but we like to use in vivo exposure whenever possible because in our experience it tends to be the more effective of the two for hoarding. However, if a person is too intimidated to do real-world exposure immediately, imaginal exposure can be used first. Following are the steps involved in E/RP. Be certain to read through the complete description of the steps before starting any actual exposure.

Step One: Construct Your Exposure Hierarchy

Before actually performing either imaginal or in vivo exposure, you will need to create a *hierarchy* of anxiety-producing situations. A hierarchy is a list of various situations that cause some degree of anxiety for you. Typically, hierarchies are presented in descending order, from the most anxiety producing to the least anxiety producing.

A hierarchy is required for E/RP because you want to tackle situations one at a time and in a manner that will help you succeed. If you just randomly exposed yourself to different situations, you probably would feel more anxious and frustrated than you would if you proceeded in a systematic and structured manner. This idea sounds familiar, right? It's the same way you did the cleanup and maintenance work: one task at a time, in a systematic and structured format. E/RP is the same; it is significantly more effective when carried out with structure.

In order to construct the hierarchy, you will need to consider the relative difficulty of the anxiety-producing situations and then rate the items in terms of how much anxiety you anticipate each of them will create. You will rate each situation using the *subjective units of distress scale,* or SUDS, which ranges from 1 to 100, with 1 being low anxiety and 100 being intense anxiety.

The following is a sample hierarchy for someone who has difficulty limiting the acquisition of new possessions.

Situation	SUDS
Going to a garage sale and not purchasing any items	100
Going to a garage sale and purchasing only one item	85
Seeing an advertisement for a garage sale and not going to it	75
Going window-shopping at the mall without purchasing anything	60

Taking no brochures from the doctor's office	50
Taking one brochure from the doctor's office	40
Canceling your subscription to several newspapers or magazines	35
Canceling your subscriptions to one newspaper or magazine	25
Going grocery shopping and not purchasing multiples of items	15

Keep in mind that some of the situations in this hierarchy may apply to you, while others won't. You are likely to have your own specific situations that create anxiety. Use the above hierarchy as a reference to help you understand how to create your own hierarchy. We will use this hierarchy as an example in our explanation of the steps involved with E/RP.

Exercise: Create Your Exposure Hierarchy

Take out your notebook and find a blank page. Here you will create your own hierarchy for your exposures. Try to think of all the different situations in which you could potentially acquire new possessions. For each situation, rate how anxious you think you will be using the SUDS scale.

Once you have given each situation a SUDS number, list the situations in descending order (highest to lowest). Try to identify at least one situation between 1 and 10, at least one between 11 and 20, and so on. This will give you a well-spaced hierarchy, and it will be easier for you to do the E/RP than if you had five situations between 71 and 80 and only three situations under 40.

Step Two: Begin with the Lowest SUDS Item

Once you have constructed your own personal hierarchy, you are ready to begin the E/RP. Begin with the item at the bottom of the list (the one with the lowest SUDS rating). With our sample hierarchy, the first situation you would expose yourself to would be going grocery shopping and not purchasing multiples of items (SUDS 15).

In vivo exposure would require you to actually go to the grocery store and restrain yourself from purchasing multiples of items. You would go through the aisles as you normally do, but put only one of each item in your cart. If you used to purchase four cans of tuna, three boxes of pasta, and two jars of sauce, then in this shopping trip you would purchase only one can of tuna, one box of pasta, and one jar of sauce.

When you practice in vivo exposure, you will feel your anxiety level rise throughout the experience. Try to monitor your anxiety level throughout the exposure and remember its highest level (we'll call this the *SUDS peak*). Notice that your anxiety rarely stays at one level consistently.

During the exposure, you need to resist all urges to acquire multiples of items. Those urges are the compulsions that will temporarily reduce the anxiety you feel but will increase your overall anxiety over time. Your anxiety level will fluctuate throughout the exposure. But eventually you will habituate to the anxiety, and the level of distress will decrease rather quickly.

If you feel that doing an in vivo exposure would be too difficult to start, you can begin with an imaginal exposure. Take about an hour and sit in a quiet room. For our sample situation, you would imagine going to the grocery store and doing the exact same things we discussed in the in vivo section.

Be as specific as you can when you imagine the shopping experience. Visualize yourself driving to the market, getting out of your car, picking a shopping cart, and walking down the aisles. Imagine the specific items you pick up, and try to actually feel yourself wanting multiples but resisting those urges. Monitor your anxiety level from time to time. Notice and remember your SUDS peak. The same thing will happen in your imaginal exposure as in the in vivo: you will habituate to the anxiety and it will dissipate by itself with time.

Step Three: Repeat That Exposure Until Your SUDS Peak Is at Least 50 Percent Less

Repeat the same exposure until your SUDS peak is at least 50 percent lower than it was initially. In this case, you would repeat going to the market and not purchasing multiples of items until your peak anxiety level is one-half what it was the first time you did the exposure. Do this the same day if possible; if not, repeat the exposure as soon as you can.

For example, if the first time you did this exposure your SUDS peaked at 30, you should repeat this exposure until your highest SUDS rating during the exposure is 15 or less. For lower-level items on the hierarchy, this rule is more difficult to apply. For instance, if your peak anxiety was a 10, it may be difficult to determine a 50 percent reduction. Just try to move on when you feel comfortable doing so.

Step Four: Go On to the Next Item

If you have been doing real-world exposures, go on to steps one to three with the next item on the hierarchy. If you have been doing imaginal exposures, try doing the same exposure in vivo. Remember, the more in vivo exposure you do, the more progress you will make.

Exercise: Begin Your E/RP

Now that you know all the steps required to perform E/RP and you have constructed a hierarchy, you are ready to begin the exposures. Good luck! Remember to proceed in a structured and systematic manner. In each situation, do your best to resist your compulsions to acquire more than one item; giving in will only make your long-term anxiety much worse.

If the anxiety is severe and really uncomfortable, of course you can give in. We don't want you to suffer. Exposures should be challenging but not painful. If your anxiety is severe, it may be a good indication that you were not ready for that level of exposure and need to do lower-level exposures first.

Keep in mind that you should be proud of yourself for trying your exposures, no matter what the outcome. You have come a long way in your recovery, and this is another valuable step.

Coping with Lapses

You have done a fabulous job ending the clutter and preparing yourself to prevent relapse. We'd like to end with a quick note about *lapses*. Lapses are slight setbacks along the way. We've taught you strategies to help you keep up your gains. Despite it all, there may be times when you get back into bad habits for a short while, and it's important to be prepared.

If a lapse occurs and you do not make immediate positive changes, a lapse may advance into a *relapse,* a longer-term setback that can be more emotionally and physically disruptive in your life. It is essentially a return to many old bad habits, and clutter may become a problem again. It is very common for hoarders to have lapses following their treatment, especially a few weeks or months after the cleanup. It has been our experience that the hoarders who learn from lapses and go back to the treatment skills are often very successful in preventing relapses, maintaining their treatment gains, and maintaining high self-confidence.

If you realize that you're having a lapse or relapse, do not panic and give up. That would be like being on a diet and having one fattening food, then deciding you will never lose the weight, so you might as well just give up. We all know people who never lose weight because the minute they cheat on a diet, they give up totally. It becomes a vicious cycle and a losing battle. However, those who get back on track immediately are able to lose weight. Having one piece of cake does not mean you should abandon your diet; you should start again right after the piece of cake.

The same is true of hoarding. If you compulsively shop one day, take note of it and decide to return all the items. If you cannot return all of them, then return everything but two items. Immediately decide what you truly need. Whatever is not essential, return right away. Do not procrastinate and put it off for the next day. If you picked up free items, decide to throw them out. Remember, you are in control. Do not let the items control you.

You are most vulnerable when you are fatigued, anxious, or under stress. That is when you have to work extra hard to avoid falling back and accumulating possessions. Thus, methods of preventing these conditions are very important. Getting exercise (even walking for ten minutes); getting enough sleep; relaxing, meditating, or doing yoga; saying no when you feel overwhelmed by outside stress; visiting friends; taking vacations: these are some ways to help prevent feeling fatigued or stressed out. Whether you use these or other activities, try to incorporate as many of them as you can into your life.

If a lapse or relapse occurs, you may want to reread this book and the exercises you completed to help inspire you to get back into the treatment mode. Make new cognitive therapy flash cards to help restore your confidence and maintain a healthy perspective.

If you wake up one morning and realize that one of your functional spaces is gone, tackle the situation immediately using the three-and-a-half-box technique. Use your cognitive therapy flash cards. Do not let lapses discourage you. Fight ahead. You fought hard to get here. You should be proud of yourself. You are now in control.

References

American Psychiatric Association. 2000. *Diagnostic and Statistical Manual of Mental Disorders,* 4th ed., text revision. Washington, D.C.: American Psychiatric Association.

Beck, J. S. 1995. *Cognitive Therapy: Basics and Beyond.* New York: Guilford Press.

Cabanac, M., and A. H. Swiergiel. 1989. Rats eating and hoarding as a function of body weight and cost of foraging. *American Physiological Society* 26:952–57.

Flament, M. F., A. Whitaker, J. L. Rapoport, M. Davies, C. Z. Berg, K. Kalikow, W. Sceery, and D. Shaffer. 1988. Obsessive-compulsive disorder in adolescence: An epidemiological study. *Journal of American Academy of Child and Adolescent Psychiatry* 27:764–71.

Frost, R. O., and R. C. Gross. 1993. The hoarding of possessions. *Behaviour Research and Therapy* 31:367–81.

Frost, R. O., and T. Hartl. 1996. A cognitive behavioral model of compulsive hoarding. *Behaviour Research and Therapy* 34:341–50.

Frost, R. O., and G. Steketee. 1998. Hoarding: Clinical aspects and treatment strategies. In *Obsessive-Compulsive Disorder: Practical*

Management, edited by M. A. Jenike, L. Baer, and W. E. Minichiello. St. Louis: Mosby.

Furby, L. 1978. Possessions: Toward a theory of their meaning and function throughout the life cycle. In *Life Span Development and Behavior* vol. 1, edited by P. B. Bates. New York: Academic Press.

Gross, N. B., and V. H. Cohn Jr. 1954. The effect of vitamin-B deficiency on the hoarding behavior of rats. *American Journal of Psychology* 67:124–28.

Karno, M., J. M. Goldin, S. B. Soreman, and M. A. Burnam. 1988. The epidemiology of obsessive-compulsive disorders in five U.S. communities. *Archives of General Psychiatry* 45:1094–99.

Keys, A., P. Brozec, A. Henschel, O. Mickelson, and H. L. Taylor. 1950. *The Biology of Human Starvation* vol. 2. St. Paul, Minn.: North Central Publisher.

Pavlov, I. 1927. *Conditioned Reflexes.* New York: Oxford University Press.

Skinner, B. F. 1938. *The Behavior of Organisms: An Experimental Analysis.* Oxford: Appleton-Century.

Warren, L. W., and J. C. Ostrom. 1988. Pack rats: World-class savers. *Psychology Today* 22:58–62.

Williams, H., R. Clarke, Y. Fashola, and G. Holt. 1998. Diogenes' syndrome in patients with intellectual disability: 'A rose by any other name'? *Journal of Intellectual Disability Research* 42:316–20.

Zajonc, R. B. 1968. Attitudinal effects of mere exposure. *Journal of Personality and Social Psychology.* Suppl. no. 9.

Fugen Neziroglu, Ph.D., ABBP, is a board-certified cognitive and behavior psychologist involved in the research and treatment of anxiety disorders, obsessive-compulsive spectrum disorders, trichotillomania, hoarding, body dysmorphic disorder, and hypochondriasis at the Bio-Behavioral Institute in Great Neck, NY. She is professor of psychology at Hofstra University in Long Island, NY, and professor of psychology at New York University. A scientist and clinician who has presented and published over 150 articles in scientific journals and written many book chapters, she is coauthor of seven books with Jose Yaryura-Tobias. She has received recognition both nationally and internationally for her research contributions in the area of obsessive-compulsive spectrum disorders. She is on the Scientific Advisory Board of the Obsessive-Compulsive Foundation.

Jerome Bubrick, Ph.D., is a behavior and cognitive psychologist specializing in the treatment of obsessive-compulsive spectrum disorders and hoarding in children and adults at Bio-Behavioral Institute in Great Neck, NY. He has given presentations and workshops on these topics, both at professional conferences and within the community. He received his Ph.D. in clinical and school psychology from Hofstra University in Long Island, NY.

Jose Yaryura-Tobias, MD, is a biological psychiatrist and an internist with over forty years experience. He is the medical director of the Bio-Behavioral Institute in Great Neck, NY; professor of psychiatry at the New York University Medical School and Cuyo National University in Mendoza, Argentina; and visiting professor at the University of Salvador, Buenos Aires, Argentina. He pioneered research in the dopamine theory of schizophrenia and the serotonin theory of obsessive-compulsive disorder. He is the author of eight books, seven of which he coauthored with Fugen Neziroglu. He has presented and published over 300 scientific articles and book chapters. He is on the scientific advisory board of the Obsessive-Compulsive Foundation and a consultant to the Bio-Behavioral Institute in Buenos Aires, Argentina. He is the founder of the Federation of Biological Psychiatry. He is also a writer of fiction and poetry.

Some Other
New Harbinger Titles

Freeing the Angry Mind, Item 4380 $14.95

Living Beyond Your Pain, Item 4097 $19.95

Transforming Anxiety, Item 4445 $12.95

Integrative Treatment for Borderline Personality Disorder, Item 4461 $24.95

Depressed and Anxious, Item 3635 $19.95

Is He Depressed or What?, Item 4240 $15.95

Cognitive Therapy for Obsessive-Compulsive Disorder, Item 4291 $39.95

Child and Adolescent Psychopharmacology Made Simple, Item 4356 $14.95

ACT* on Life Not on Anger, Item 4402 $14.95

Overcoming Medical Phobias, Item 3872 $14.95

Acceptance & Commitment Therapy for Anxiety Disorders, Item 4275 $58.95

The OCD Workbook, Item 4224 $19.95

Neural Path Therapy, Item 4267 $14.95

Overcoming Obsessive Thoughts, Item 3813 $14.95

The Interpersonal Solution to Depression, Item 4186 $19.95

Get Out of Your Mind & Into Your Life, Item 4259 $19.95

Dialectical Behavior Therapy in Private Practice, Item 4208 $54.95

The Anxiety & Phobia Workbook, 4th edition, Item 4135 $19.95

Loving Someone with OCD, Item 3295 $15.95

Overcoming Animal & Insect Phobias, Item 3880 $12.95

Overcoming Compulsive Washing, Item 4054 $14.95

Angry All the Time, Item 3929 $13.95

Handbook of Clinical Psychopharmacology for Therapists, 4th edition,
    Item 3996 $55.95

Writing For Emotional Balance, Item 3821 $14.95

Surviving Your Borderline Parent, Item 3287 $14.95

When Anger Hurts, 2nd edition, Item 3449 $16.95

Calming Your Anxious Mind, Item 3384 $12.95

Ending the Depression Cycle, Item 3333 $17.95

Call **toll free, 1-800-748-6273,** or log on to our online bookstore at **www.newharbinger.com** to order. Have your Visa or Mastercard number ready. Or send a check for the titles you want to New Harbinger Publications, Inc., 5674 Shattuck Ave., Oakland, CA 94609. Include $4.50 for the first book and 75¢ for each additional book, to cover shipping and handling. (California residents please include appropriate sales tax.) Allow two to five weeks for delivery.

Prices subject to change without notice.